T0051205

Praise for *Secrets from Chuckling Goat*:

'From Brynhoffnant to Fortnum & Mason – an impressive story of risk and determination, but ultimately one of human fulfilment. This deeply personal story of a Ceredigion farm and its inhabitants will strike a chord with many families across rural Britain. And as for Chuckling Goat's many products – I am a convinced convert!'
MARK WILLIAMS, MEMBER OF PARLIAMENT FOR CEREDIGION

'Shann Jones describes an almost magical journey from high-flying journalist to goat farmer and natural products entrepreneur. The book is a very powerful illustration of the healing powers of natural products, positive thinking and hard work!'
PROFESSOR TOM HUMPHREY, PROFESSOR OF BACTERIOLOGY AND FOOD SAFETY, SWANSEA UNIVERSITY

'I have enjoyed this book very much! It is written with wonderful warmth and humour. It is a story of revelation, transformation and discovery of the essence of life itself. I warmly recommend it!'
DR NATASHA CAMPBELL-MCBRIDE MMEDSCI(NEUROLOGY), MMEDSCI(NUTRITION) AND AUTHOR OF GUT AND PSYCHOLOGY SYNDROME

'This book is a refreshing reminder that the secret to the universe is always right in front of us. Shann's book reads like a sleigh ride through the countryside and every page reveals a new landscape that delights our senses. An epic journey of one woman's belief in her ability to rediscover the wisdom in nature and the goodness of life while facing the most daunting of circumstances.'
PETER MEYERS, PRESIDENT, STAND & DELIVER CONSULTING GROUP, GLOBAL COMMUNICATION AND LEADERSHIP CONSULTING

'Secrets from Chuckling Goat is a compelling account of one woman's remarkable journey. Shann's is an engaging, and at times poignant, tale of her life with Rich and their "blended" family, as they face the joys and sorrows of making a living from the land and developing a new goats' milk enterprise. Shann chances to discover the healing properties of goats' milk products, which, as well as saving Rich's life, also launches her business into the world of natural medicine. This heart-warming account of finding true love in the face of adversity, and the healing properties of goats' milk, is laced with a good measure of human kindness – I commend it to you.'
WILLIAM POWELL, LIBERAL DEMOCRAT ASSEMBLY MEMBER FOR MID- AND WEST WALES, SHADOW MINISTER FOR FOOD AND FARMING, NATIONAL ASSEMBLY FOR WALES

Secrets from
CHUCKLING
GOAT

Secrets from

CHUCKLING
GOAT

How a herd of goats saved my family
and started a business that became
a natural health phenomenon

SHANN NIX JONES

HAY HOUSE

Carlsbad, California • New York City
London • Sydney • New Delhi

Library of Congress Control Number: 2014955950

Tradepaper ISBN: 978-1-4019-6944-8

1st edition, February 2015

Printed in the United States of America

For Rich, who promised me that he would stay... and did.

'It may be that when we no longer know what to do,
we have come to our real work
and when we no longer know which way to go,
we have begun our real journey.'
WENDELL BERRY, NOVELIST, POET, ENVIRONMENTAL ACTIVIST AND FARMER

Foreword

As someone who is passionate about natural products, I first came across Chuckling Goat when I received a sample of their gorgeous goats' milk soap. I got to know the lovely Shann, and indeed I think it's fair to say I encouraged her to write this book. It was clear she had a fascinating story. I'm delighted I did so – it's a fabulous read.

The book opens with Shann in her 'former life' as a news journalist and talk show host in America, leading a fast-paced, cut-throat existence. It's hard to believe it's not fiction when you read of her transformation to 'mistress of a 25-acre farm', creator of the most gorgeous skincare products and 'healer' – in more ways than one.

The book is entertaining, moving, thought provoking and educational. Prepare to be amazed as Shann shares her knowledge of the benefits of goats' milk and goats' milk kefir – nature's miracle, which can repopulate our guts with good flora and keep us healthy.

Going back to a traditional way of eating, Shann and her family stumbled upon some truths. She says, 'Like learning to co-exist with the world outside, we have to learn to co-exist with the world inside – all the trillions of tiny living cells living on us and in us without which we could not exist. We are the planet. Literally.'

She shares time-honoured recipes, too – interspersed through her story are recipes for pineapple marmalade, rye sourdough bread and, of course, goats' milk kefir.

Shann's passion for her goats, her goats' milk kefir and her family (not necessarily in that order!) really shines through. I can imagine this being made into a movie – I know she'll insist on leading the goats down the red carpet!

JANEY LEE GRACE
AUTHOR AND MENTOR FOR HOLISTIC PROFESSIONALS

x

I must be the luckiest woman in the world.

I stand at my kitchen sink and look over the sunlit valley stretching out towards the ocean. The bracken is just beginning to change colour, adding rust to the patchwork quilt of the hills. In the distance, a tiny wisp of smoke escapes from the chimney of a white farmhouse. The clouds cast shadows over the cultivated fields and hedges, the rough gold alternating with tidy patches of green where the hay has been mown.

Our own hay has been cut and baled, and I hold that fact in the back of my mind with the satisfaction of a squirrel contemplating its seasonal store of nuts. Rich went round and round the field on his tractor – mowing, turning, rowing and finally baling the hay during a lucky burst of bright sun, late in the summer. The whole family turned out to throw the bales onto the trailer, and then rode the wobbling load back into the shed, where we stacked it, fragrant and neat, ready for winter.

Our goats will eat this hay through the winter, giving us their magical milk to make into healing probiotic drinks, soaps and skin creams.

There's a deep calm and contentment in my farmhouse kitchen, with its long scrubbed wooden table, the blue enamel Alpha range cooker humming in the corner, the apple-green walls framing the huge picture window looking out to the sea. In the corner, there's an earthenware bowl full of milk and rennet, setting for cheese.

There's a Kilner jar of goat's milk kefir working on the counter, and a bowl of sourdough bread rising. Simmering on the stove is a pan of the traditional Welsh stew called 'cawl', along with one of my own inventions, a sweet (bell) pepper chutney that the kids have dubbed Pecka Pickled Peppers.

The entire bottom shelf of the refrigerator is full of milk from the goats – the two beauties that we're milking at the moment give us close to 6 litres (10.5 pints) a day. That's enough milk to experiment with, to try things with, and to feed the pigs. More than enough. It's riches – wealth.

The hay in the barn makes me feel wealthy, too – it's enough to keep our goats well fed and healthy, without having to buy it from anyone. We know exactly what's gone into our hay – it's free from chemicals and full of herbs and flowers and seed heads, like the most marvellous kind of potpourri.

I love to feed our hay to the goats – I love to watch them pulling it in contented mouthfuls out of the wooden hay rack that Rich made for them. Their coats are smooth and glossy, their long, almond-shaped eyes seductive. I lean my head against their warm flanks when I milk them, and smell their sweet breath as the milk foams into the jug under my hands. Riches. Happiness.

I love my computer, too; it's a fantastic, flexible tool. But it doesn't make me happy.

In fact, the more time I spend in front of the screen, the more jittery and empty I feel. The reason for this was once explained to me by Jaron Lanier, the computer science visionary who invented virtual reality.

In 1991, decades ago and worlds away from this serene farmhouse kitchen, I was a cub reporter in the USA, at the *San Francisco Chronicle* newspaper. For one of my very first assignments, I was sent down to California's Silicon Valley to interview Lanier. (This was back in the days before anyone had experienced the simulated, 3-D environment of virtual reality.)

I waited in an empty conference room until the door opened, and Lanier walked in. He was tubby and unhealthily pale, with wild reddish dreadlocks and eyes that showed the whites all the way around. His tie-dyed T-shirt was faintly grubby.

Lanier explained his invention to me. Virtual reality, he said, was an entire world existing inside the computer, with which you could engage as fully as you chose. (This was the original, high-octane version – not the watered-down one that would later hit the computer software shelves.) When wearing the full virtual reality suit, complete with headphones and goggles, you'd be completely plunged into the world of your choice, be it a castle, a desert, a moon station or a submarine.

You could choose a 'body' to wear – a lobster, say, – and then move it as if it were your own. So, if you looked down at your arm, you'd see a lobster's claw. Your choice of body was as infinite as your choice of setting. You could be a warrior, a space monster, a princess, a demon – whatever you liked.

Once these initial decisions had been made, you were free to play. You existed inside the virtual world, as fully as you did in the real world. You could turn corners, walk, run, leap over walls. And here's the real kicker – other people could meet you there. If someone in Tokyo logged on wearing similar apparatus, you'd see their virtual self appear in the setting with you – looking however they'd chosen to appear. You could interact with them, even though their physical body was across the ocean.

And then – if you got bored – with the sweep of a virtual paintbrush, you could erase your entire world and start over. Dump the moon station and set up a mossy bank by a river. Get rid of your demon outfit and change into a hawk. There was no limit to the possibilities except your imagination. Needless to say, the military was interested.

After I was sure that I'd understood the unbelievable parameters of what Lanier was telling me, I asked the pressing question that had just occurred to me: 'Aren't you worried that people will get addicted to this virtual reality? If they can look any way they want, in any world they choose, why wouldn't they just stay inside the computer world forever?'

Lanier shook his head. 'They won't,' he said. 'For one reason – texture.'

'Texture?' I asked, baffled.

'I can make the world inside a computer look any way you want it to look,' he went on. 'I can create any scenario. I can make things move the way you want them to move. But I can't put texture inside a computer.' He knocked on the wood of the meeting table. 'I can't make you feel the hardness of wood, or the softness of leather, or the wetness of water. At least... not yet.' He cracked a radiant, lopsided, mad-genius grin.

'And it turns out that we need texture. We crave it, because we're biological animals. And that's why no-one will stay inside a computer forever.' He sounded vaguely regretful.

I thanked Lanier and drove back to the newspaper office to write my story. It ran. I went on to write other stories. But his words about texture always lingered in my head, as something important. I didn't understand exactly *how* important until many years later.

I worked at the newspaper for five more years, and then went into radio, diving cleanly into the surreal, icy-plastic world of American media. The day that I was hired as a talk show host at San Francisco's number one radio station, my new boss leaned towards me and shook my hand over the polished oval table in the conference room. He stared at me with hard blue eyes.

'I want you to dance on the high wire,' he said. 'I want to feel like you're always about to fall off. If you really fall off, I'll fire you. And I can't tell you where the edge is. Good luck.'

This radio station had dominated the ratings for decades. And this particular job had only come open because my predecessor had thrown himself off the Golden Gate Bridge at three in the afternoon, in the midst of busy traffic.

Wilfully closing my eyes to the implications of this fact, I cleared the dead man's sticky desk, threw away his photographs, emptied his littered drawers and bought a small, spiky pot plant to settle any restless lingering spirits. I was on my way.

Every night as thousands of San Franciscans streamed home from work, I drove the opposite way, into the city to man the night shift on the radio. I worked at night and slept during the day. I sat in a glass booth and spoke to invisible listeners. Heavy, soundproofed doors opened and closed; red on-air lights whirled in the long beige hallways. We were meant to become 'personalities' – arrogant and wildly eccentric. Diva-style temper tantrums were not only expected but actively encouraged.

During a televised fundraising drive, I accepted a dare to shave off all my hair if the listener pledges reached £275,000. They did, and I did – my mother was watching the TV, and dropped her bag of groceries when she saw me sitting there, long strands of curly hair dropping onto the floor beneath the electric razor.

The following day I sauntered into my boss's office, bald head gleaming, wearing a leather motorcycle jacket. Well pleased with myself, I slumped into his armchair and put my boots up on his desk. He stared at me.

'Your problem is that you're too cool for school,' he remarked. 'What you need is a couple of kids and a mortgage. A few dings in your fender.'

But that didn't happen – not for 10 long years. Ten years of hosting my own talk show with over a million listeners a night; 10 years of making myself tough enough to survive the high wire. All that pared me down to a wintry, sinewy set of muscles – I could argue, I could debate and I could entertain – but very little else.

I drove a convertible; I lived in an apartment with a wraparound view of San Francisco Bay, and hired a maid to clean it for me. I couldn't boil an egg, or iron a shirt. It never occurred to me that I'd ever need to.

And then, one day, my boss called me into his office.

'Be quick,' I said. 'I'm on the air in five minutes.'

'No, you're not,' he said. 'Your show's just been cancelled.'

I walked out of his office in a daze. I felt cold and numb. But there was something else, too – a strange sense of relief. There weren't a lot of career opportunities for a radio talk show host who'd already worked at the biggest station in the area, and whose major talent was making a million people angry, all at the same time. But I was strangely placid in the midst of my fear. Something would come for me – *something* would turn up. I just didn't know what.

What turned up wasn't a job, but a person. A British man on holiday in California. We fell abruptly in love, with the kind of thunderclap that you read about in books, and he took me and my four-year-old daughter back to England with him. We got married. We moved together to Wales. And after that, let's just say things turned very dark.

Five years later, I packed a suitcase, walked out of his front door and drove away – jobless, homeless and friendless, with my two children sobbing in the back seat of the car.

I spent the next two years living in a stone cottage in this strange country, along with my kids, Joli and Benji. I got my water from a well and dried my laundry on a washing line. There were no neighbours in sight – just a lot of sheep that we could see through the big picture window. We marvelled at the tidy organization and social structure of the herd. It was better than a nature documentary.

'Come back to California,' my mother urged me every time we spoke on the phone. 'Come home.'

I shook my head stubbornly during these conversations, even though she couldn't see me.

'I *am* home,' I insisted. And somehow, even though things were lonely and difficult, it seemed true. Wales held me – it possessed a power over me that I couldn't define. There was something for me in those misty hills; something that I couldn't yet decipher or see, but it drew me and held me all the same.

This was a place with silver rivers running through it like arterial blood, where clouds of sheep drifted over distant hills and castles surged up in the middle of stony towns. This place where I was a stranger, where I didn't speak the language, where the sky was always grey, where a sense of pure, cold wildness welled up like a spring in my footprints – I didn't want to leave this place.

There was something elusive and shimmering here, just below the surface. The landscape seemed to me to be assembled with infinite tender significance. It meant something. The soft froth of the beeches and alders and wych elms; the grey-fingered hazel growing along the hedgerows, dividing the green velvet fields into chess squares; the white farmhouses with their definitive, storybook plumes of smoke – these things whispered secrets to me, things that I couldn't quite hear.

I'd been plunged into a world as alien to me as one of Jaron Lanier's virtual-reality environments. Here, the houses were made of stone, and the streets were only wide enough for one car. The butcher, the fruit and veg shop and the haberdashery closed at noon on Wednesday, and all day on Sunday.

There were no billboards, no advertisements, no plastic of any kind. Only endless mist, distant hills, ruined castles and cottages painted the colour of emeralds, heather and jonquils. Weathered old men wearing muddy Wellington boots and plaid flat caps – trailed by black-and-white sheep dogs – herded bleating lambs to market in the centre of town.

I lived alone with my children in this strange new world, and it began to feel as though I always would. My chances of meeting anyone seemed to be nil – all I ever did was the school run, and the grocery-store run. Everyone I met seemed already firmly knitted into existing family structures.

As a single woman and an American I was too noticeable to fit in, and too suspect to blend. In California, I might have ventured out solo or with girlfriends, but in traditional Wales, a decent single woman doesn't go to the pub alone, and in any case, I wasn't interested in a partner who frequented pubs all the time.

'You should go online,' a dear friend from California said, when calling to check up on me. 'Have a look at one of those online dating services.' He also suggested that I could make a bit of money from home by doing some writing for people who wanted to enhance their profile.

Why not? I thought. So, a little nervously, I fired up the computer and logged onto a dating website. What a hoot! Shopping for a partner suddenly seemed as easy as shopping for shoes. Type in the marital background and educational history you want, plus the height, weight and physical characteristics. Then decide on tattoos or no tattoos? Children or no children? Earning power? Religious background? The choices are endless.

The writing exercises required to fill out a profile were a revelation to me. What did I want in a partner? I'd never really stopped to think. I'd simply been yanked this way and that by my heart – which was impulsive and never particularly clever, as it turned out – and had followed wherever it led. Now I was getting my brain involved, for the first time. I sat down and made a list.

After my previous experiences, I knew that I wanted someone gentle. Someone kind. Someone who loved children and animals – someone with children of his own. I wanted someone capable and smart and funny – someone strong and humorous who wasn't afraid of getting his hands dirty.

I entered my profile, worked out my wish list, wrote up my details, and before I'd even uploaded my picture, there was a 'ping' from an e-mail in my inbox. It was from a man named Rich who lived in a nearby town – a harp maker and woodworker with two children of his own.

We e-mailed back and forth a bit, and I mentioned idly that my daughter Joli had just been performing in the local eisteddfod, the Welsh competition for singing and poetry. *'Da lawn, Joli!'* (Well done, Joli!) came the enthusiastic reply. He asked loads of questions about the event.

I was taken aback; I was unaccustomed to having keen interest displayed in my children. I'd been a single mother for such a long time, used to sitting at school events looking straight ahead and trying not to shrink from my awareness of the solid, happy family units all around me.

Would I like to speak on the phone? Rich asked. Or would that make me uncomfortable? (Looking back, it makes me laugh – because even then, he knew what made me tick. Of course, I'm not scared to talk on the phone! Me? Scared? I picked up the phone straight away.)

And once I heard his voice, I was hooked. Rich has a deep, lazy voice and a pirate's laugh. A passionate Welshman born and bred, his family come from a long line of Welsh kings, shipwreckers and smugglers.

After a few days, the question came – did I want to meet for lunch? I agreed. I drove past the café once, so nervous that I nearly kept driving. But I parked and went in. Rich was sitting at a table facing the door. He looked up and smiled at me.

And that was that.

I was 41 years old before I really fell in love properly. And I had more baggage and miscellaneous life experience behind me than any one woman should really have. But I can tell you this – it was worth the wait.

Rich was tall and broad-shouldered, with woodworker's hands and green eyes. We talked as if we'd always known each other. We talked until the lunch service was over – all the food had gone by the time we got round to ordering. They closed the café up around us.

He told me that his two teenage daughters lived with him, and that their mother had left the year before. I told him about my two children, then aged two and nine. We exchanged war stories about being single parents.

For our first proper date, he invited me and my children over to his place for a family dinner. As I knocked nervously on the door of the big, rambling old stone farmhouse, I admired the long sweeping view of the sea.

Rich's daughters, Ceris and Elly, were both beautiful, sweet-faced and very slender, one blonde and one brunette. They were lovely with my little two, sweeping them into the lounge to play.

Rich proceeded to expertly dish up a delicious roast dinner. I watched him, impressed with the way he handled the heavy dishes and very gently moved one of the children out of the way to reach the stove. I'd forgotten what a man who is both strong and gentle looks like.

We had a wonderful time on that family first date. Next I invited Rich and his girls back to my little cottage for supper. I cooked roast chicken, which was just about the only thing I knew how to make at the time! Luckily for me, Rich's eldest daughter Ceris adores chicken!

We made Easter eggs that day, blowing the insides out of the eggs, colouring them with wax and dyeing them with bright colours. We still have those Easter eggs, now carefully tucked inside one of the traditional Welsh wooden dressers that Rich made from a tree he cut down on his parent's property.

We carried on in this way for some time. I'm not sure that Rich and I were ever really alone – we were nearly always surrounded by some combination of our four children. It was lovely.

Finally, Ceris and Elly texted me, asking if we – me, Joli and Benji – would move in with them and their dad.

I phoned Rich. 'Did you put them up to this?'

'No,' he said. 'It was their idea. I think they liked the chicken you cooked.'

I talked it over with my children, and they were thrilled with the idea. We accepted. And so we all moved to the farm. I was thrilled, too. Not only had I – finally! – met and fallen in love with the man of my dreams, but it had also always been a dream of mine to live on a farm. It was a misty sort of dream, mind, one in which I wore floating Laura Ashley dresses and skipped down the hill in a wide-brimmed hat, carrying a shiny bucket and gathering flowers.

The reality, as I was about to discover, was very different.

The farm is a traditional Welsh smallholding, perched on top of a hill looking over the Irish Sea. On a clear day, so Rich's father told me, you can see all the way to Ireland. This is South West Wales, however, so there have only been about two clear days in the past 15 years. (Wales specializes in fog, rain and the kind of floating mist that made it a model for J.R.R. Tolkien's magical kingdoms.

The saturated environment produces a lush green grass – immortalized by Welsh singer Tom Jones in the song 'Green, Green Grass of Home' – that makes the UK a world leader in sheep and goat production.)

Here, Rich lived with the girls, and his father, Taid. (His much-beloved mother, Biddy, had lived with them until her death 10 years before.) They kept chickens and sheep, and a few pigs from time to time.

When I first met him, Rich worked as a harp maker in the Harp Centre of Wales – he's a master woodworker. His hands are big, rough and scarred, with a surprisingly delicate touch. These are hands that can cut down a tree, saw up the wood and turn it into a breathtaking Welsh dresser; weld any kind of metal; create nearly any type of farm implement out of bits of scrap and baler twine; deliver a lamb, and wield a rifle with lethal accuracy. (The only thing Rich can't handle is plastic – he's hopeless at opening rubbish bags or the flimsy see-through bags in grocery stores, which forces him to ask passing pretty ladies for help. Or so he tells me.)

They are also hands that are completely comfortable with slaughtering, skinning and butchering an animal. There's no room for squeamishness on a farm, and the Welsh tradition is ultimately practical. They value above all else the ability to 'get on with it'.

The Welsh traditionally built cottages that they could raise, with the help of friends and neighbours, in one night of heavy beer drinking. If they could have smoke coming out of the chimney by morning, the cottage was theirs. They claimed their land by throwing an axe as far from the new doorstep as they could manage – which is why many farms have a long, narrow field running down from the farmhouse. Easier to throw downhill than uphill!

The traditional Welsh cottage has tiny windows because the Welsh are less worried about admiring the stunning landscape that surrounds them than they are about surviving the never-ending battle with the cold and damp. It's a country that has been economically depressed since the English invaded back in the eleventh century – with a cultural heritage that's passionate, intricate and completely unique.

The Welsh hold a massive, nationally televised competition every year to establish the finest singer, dancer, actor and poet in the land. Thousands of men, women and children compete in this artistic Olympics, which is called the National Eisteddfod of Wales, flocking to inhabit a temporary tent village that's set up for this very purpose during an entire celebratory week.

In nearly every district in the country, in a tradition dating from the time of the druids, they still robe and 'chair' a Bard every year, leading the winning poet to sit on a wooden throne in an elaborate ceremony involving a real sword.

When forced into the mines to feed their families, the Welsh men had a response that awes me every time I think of it – they lifted up their voices and sang. The miners created an exquisite tradition of Welsh male choirs that thrives to this day, although the mines have long since shut down.

All these details and more, I was about to discover. Why? Because suddenly, abruptly, and with no warning or training, I was the mistress of a 10-hectare (25-acre) farm.

This meant that I was responsible for a large and cluttered farmhouse kitchen, dominated by a 2.5-metre (8-foot) long kitchen table (made by Rich) around which as many as 10 people might gather at meal times, looking at me expectantly, ready for food.

No-one here gave a damn that I'd once written for a newspaper and worked in radio. They cared only whether or not I could make a 'good cup of tea', bake a tray of scones, cook the traditional cawl, make homemade faggots out of pig's liver and lights (lungs) and put together a roast dinner on a Sunday afternoon – all the requisites for Welsh farm life. And of course, I couldn't do any of those things!

In California I'd had a load of restaurants nearby, and a convertible to drive to them. Learning to cook had just never been a priority. But now, stranded in my strange new life, pride and desperation drove me to try. With a battered copy of the *Complete Farmhouse Cookbook* in hand, I tied on an apron, gritted my teeth and began to produce disasters.

I'd been on this kind of learning curve before. When I first came to the UK from America, six years before, there had been more challenges than just learning to drive on the wrong side of the road, in the wrong side of the car, gear-shifting with the wrong hand.

For example, I'd discovered to my grief that a cup of tea isn't *just* a cup of tea. There's a good cup of tea, and a not-so-good cup of tea. I'd set a timer, testing the tea each time until I worked out that three minutes is the perfect length of time to leave it – strong enough, but still boiling hot.

The next thing I had to master was that mysterious thing the British call a 'roast dinner'. We don't have these in the USA; in fact, we don't have anything that everyone eats on the same day. Americans simply don't have traditional foods the way the British do – except on Thanksgiving.

But I worked out that this 'roast dinner' has a pretty set menu. There's some kind of roast meat – possibly chicken but more often beef, lamb or pork. And each meat is accompanied by a specific sauce: mint sauce with lamb, apple sauce with pork. With beef you have mustard and Yorkshire pudding – whatever that was.

Always roast potatoes, too. Oh, the minefield of roast potatoes. They must be crispy on the outside, floury on the inside. It's not just a dish but a cult – to the point that farm wives actually take their roast potatoes to fairs to be judged.

Creating a dish of crispy roast potatoes wasn't the worst bit, though. I finally cracked those when I learned to boil the potatoes – and they must be the right type, preferably Maris Piper – for exactly eight minutes, then drain them, put the lid back on the pan and then shake it in a rib-crunching bout until the surfaces get all rough and ragged, then tip the potatoes into a roasting pan with boiling hot oil on the bottom, then into the oven for an hour. Sorted – as the Welsh say about a job well done.

No, the roast potatoes weren't the worst bit – the worse bit was mastering the Yorkshire pudding. Ah, the agonies of the

Yorkshire pudding. Each one I made was flatter and soggier than the one before, and I couldn't work out what I was doing wrong. Put two spoonfuls of beef dripping in the pan, the recipe said, heat that up and then pour in the Yorkshire pudding batter. It 'should' rise up golden and puffy. Mine just lay there, pale and flabby, like a wet week.

Until the day that I was wandering through the grocery store, looking for clues, and I saw something on the shelf that made my jaw drop. Beef dripping. It's a product that you buy! A grease product, like lard or suet. We don't have it in the USA, and so I'd just been taking two spoonfuls of the water from the roasting tray to cook my Yorkshires in. Aha...

Now, living with Rich's family, it was time for me to master a whole new list of mysterious dishes. I learned to close my eyes and put my hands into a huge bowl of mushed-up raw pork, to mix it with sage and onion for stuffing. I slowly became adept at boiling up huge vats of meat broth with vegetables, in order to make cawl. I even learned to heat up the ancient cast-iron griddle, called a bake stone, that had once belonged to Rich's mother, to make proper Welsh cakes, with butter rubbed into flour.

I learned other things, as well. I learned to grow tomatoes. I shaved the bristles off a dead pig. I chucked hay bales and drove a tractor. I dug in the mud, got sweaty and dirty, worked till I was physically exhausted and tried to master all the antique skills that women once learned as soon as they could walk.

And one day I stood with my elbows on the gate, looking out over the hills, and I felt an unfamiliar feeling.

I was happy.

I felt peaceful, contented, serene. Alive. Feelings I couldn't remember having had in all the plastic hustle of my former life.

Lanier was right. The secret was texture.

My life in Wales wasn't fast-paced or high-powered, but it was loaded with texture. The smooth-worn wood of the old rolling pin, the weight of the heavy cast-iron frying pan, the sharp scent of the rosemary growing outside the kitchen window – these things rooted and grounded me, woke me up, connected me, made me feel, made me want to be alive – made me *glad* to be alive.

These things created a super-charged sensation that was texture and even more – something I would come to call 'textureality'.

I could see that my previous life, with all its fast pace and labour-saving devices, had been stripped of many of the things that made me now feel content and whole – in the same way that the bleached, featureless white dust that we call 'flour' is stripped of any nutrition and fibre.

The old tasks of growing food, baking bread, making jam, tending animals – we were designed by thousands of years of evolution to do these jobs, to interact with the natural world in a mutually beneficial way. There was a huge, silent, internal satisfaction when I finally began to do the things I was designed to do.

I took the vegetable scraps to the pigs. When the pigs were big enough, we slaughtered them and made sausages and roasts. The pig dung went onto the compost pile, and the finished compost went into the polytunnel – where the vegetables grow.

I harvested the vegetables, cooked them, served them to my family – and took the new scraps out to the pigs. A connected, richly textural cycle.

There wasn't a lot of texture left in my previous processed, plasticized, pre-packed, sanitized city life. Plop me into a sterile cubicle in front of a computer all day, and then shove me into an air-conditioned car to get home, where I eat a microwaved meal and sit in front of the television until it's time to go to sleep – there's no texture in that. I'd been slowly starving, because I was deprived of texture, and I need it.

In my efforts to live as leisurely a life as possible, I'd outsourced many of the things that actually gave me the greatest satisfaction. Other people grew my vegetables, milked cows to provide my milk, made my bread, and put my jam into jars, depriving me of the deep textural contentment that these tasks bring. I'd literally thrown a lot of critically important babies out with the bath water.

As a biological creature, I *need* this texture. I crave it. I've not (yet?) evolved to the point where I can be truly happy without it. Perhaps I never will. Technology alone just doesn't do it for me. There was a nagging, jittery emptiness that comes from the lack of texture in modern life, and I'd just tried to fill it by going faster and buying more stuff. And for me, it simply never worked.

Textureality is hot, cold, hard, wet, soft, warm. It's leather and mud, wood and stone. It's sinking your hands into the dirt, digging with a shovel until your arms ache, taking a walk in the rain and coming back inside for a cup of really hot tea. It's wrapping a cashmere blanket around your child, cooking in a heavy iron frying pan, crushing a stalk of lavender under your nose and inhaling the heavenly scent. It's simmering a pot of homemade soup on the stove all day, so that it perfumes the air and becomes, over time, something that even scientists agree has healing properties.

Textureality has to do with slow magic. It takes time to plant a tomato seed, to water it and watch it grow, to pick the tomatoes and eat them, to compost the plant at the end of the season. But it's rich, fulfilling, satisfying, and it brings contentment. In the same way that food that you really have to chew is better for you, so I discovered that my life began to nourish me once I put some of the ancient textures back into it.

The alchemical transformation of disparate bits of water, meat and vegetables into a rich stew – that's slow magic. The rising process of yeast transforming flour and sugar into bread – more slow magic. Watching a skein of wool turn into a scarf, or a piece of wood turn into a spoon under your hands – that's magic, as well.

And it produces happiness, and cures boredom. I've never heard an avid gardener, or a horsewoman, or a quilter, complain of boredom. For these people, there are never enough hours in the day. They are deeply engaged with processes that feed their spirit. They have textureality in their lives, and their lives are enriched. People who follow a craft, who grow things, who interact with animals, who make things from scratch, all draw from the well of this ancient alchemical magic.

Mind you, we're not completely antique on the farm. Nor would we choose to be. I'm more than grateful to live in an age of technological marvels, vaccinations and running water – where

I have the luxury of drifting back through previous decades and centuries, cherry-picking the bits I prefer.

I can do my grocery shopping online, and spend the free afternoon I gain making my own blackberry jam. Not because it's quick, or easy (although making jam is a lot easier than I used to think!) but because the process itself is intensely pleasurable and it makes me feel good.

Real comfort food, I discovered, was not empty calories that I ingested and immediately regretted, but traditional farmhouse dishes that comforted me in the making of them. The process itself – baking the bread, making the pies, stirring the jam – was where the comfort was hidden. Happiness and serenity were waiting for me, decanted like the glistening dark blood of the blackberries, hidden in the tasks of the past.

For me, it has to do with a sense of place. There's a certain and specific magic in this place, and the magic is mined by interacting with it – by planting, by milking the goats that eat the plants, by turning the milk into food that we eat, soap that we use to wash ourselves. There's a crystalline beauty to the interaction of each piece of this puzzle that actually does create elation.

~~~~~~~~~~

Best of all there were the goats.

The goats came about in a strange way.

It all started, as these things so often do, with a need. Both Rich and I value family above everything else, and we'd do anything to keep our family safe and healthy. So when there's a medical challenge, we set out to fix it, using the tools that the farm gives us – nature, our animals, our pots and pans and the farmhouse kitchen table.

So really, the story of the goats begins with the day that I took Benji, as a toddler, to see a doctor, to check a nasty chest infection.

The doctor listened through his stethoscope and looked at me over Benji's head.

'Bronchiolitis,' he said briefly.

'Is that serious?' I asked.

'I'm afraid it is.' He picked up the phone. 'Ambulance to the front door, right away, please,' he said into the handset.

He rapidly stripped off all my son's clothes and thrust him back into my arms, dressed only in his nappy.

'Run,' he said. 'The ambulance will be waiting by the door.'

'But it's December. It's freezing out there,' I said stupidly.

'His temperature is too high,' the doctor said. 'Run.'

I ran.

Benji had always had bronchial infections, asthma and eczema. He got congested easily and once he caught a cold, the infection would settle into his lungs. We were forced to give him dose after dose of antibiotics, and the problem just seemed to get worse every time.

On this occasion, he stayed in the hospital overnight. And as I hovered over him, unable to relieve his laboured breathing, I determined that we were going to do something – anything – to change things.

'What can we do?' I asked Rich. By this time I had unshakable faith in him – I asked him things, and he always knew the answer. He didn't fail me this time, either.

'We need a goat,' he said.

'A goat? Why?'

I'd never kept goats – or animals of any sort, really, apart from the odd dog. But I was desperate, and ready to try anything. Rich had kept goats before, when his girls were young, and knew of the traditional reputation of goat's milk for easing allergies, asthma and chest infections.

So, after another particularly harrowing appointment with the GP, during which Benji was yet again stuck full of antibiotics, we drove directly from the surgery into the hills around South West Wales, to see a man who had a goat for sale.

We took lovely black-and-white Buddug the goat home in the trailer, and I learned how to milk her that very night. We gave Benji a glass of the goat's milk, holding our breath. He drank it straight down – and smiled up at us.

I later discovered that the reason goat's milk is helpful for people suffering from asthma, bronchial conditions and eczema is because it's much less likely to cause an allergic reaction than cow's milk. An allergic reaction can be blamed on a protein allergen known as Alpha s1 Casein, which is found in high levels in cow's milk. The levels of Alpha s1 Casein in goat's milk are about 89 per cent lower than in cow's milk – providing a far less allergenic food.

Goat's milk is also naturally homogenized. If you put a glass of goat's milk and a glass of cow's milk in the fridge overnight, you'll find that the cow's milk separates into a thick layer of cream on top and skim milk on the bottom – a natural process caused by something called agglutinin.

To prevent this separation, the dairy industry uses a process called homogenization, which forces the fluid milk through a small hole under pressure. This destroys the fat globule cell walls and allows the milk and cream to stay suspended and well mixed. The problem with homogenization is that once the cell wall of the fat globule has been broken, it releases a free radical known as Xanthine Oxidase. Free radicals can cause problems in the body, including DNA mutations that can lead to cancer.

Goat's milk, on the other hand, is closer in molecular composition to human milk. It has smaller fat globules and contains no agglutinin, which allows it to stay naturally homogenized. It also contains less lactose than cow's milk and is, therefore, easier to digest for those suffering from lactose intolerance.

Five years later, Benji's frightening chest infections are a thing of the past. He's strong and fit, rarely catches a cold and hasn't needed antibiotics in years. His asthma inhalers are gathering dust in the cupboard.

When we had too much goat's milk to drink, I began looking for things to do with the excess – and discovered goat's milk soap. Then I learned to put the milk into handmade skin cream as well. I used it on Benji, and his eczema disappeared. Soon, mothers on the school run began asking me for our goat's milk soap and skin cream, for their own children who had eczema. We bought another goat, and then another. And we now own – and milk – an entire herd of goats!

~~~~~~~~~

My daughter Joli was a vegetarian when we moved to the farm. She'd come to me when she was six, and announced that she'd no longer eat animals. 'It's wrong,' she'd told me seriously, and looking into her eyes, I couldn't argue.

'I'll support you,' I said. 'But I'm still going to eat meat myself.'

The truth is that I'm a Texas girl who loves a good steak. I've simply never had the inclination to become a vegetarian. I'm full of respect – and even awe – for those who are. It's beyond impressive to me, to live a life in which you never succumb to the smell of bacon.

But I did support Joli in her intention to become a vegetarian, researching carefully to ensure that the meat-free meals I cooked her were nutritionally balanced and healthy. She never once wavered. For three years, no meat crossed her six-, seven- and eight- year-old lips. She seemed quite happy and settled in her resolve, and I became an expert in the offerings of Quorn.

So I wasn't sure how my little daughter's philosophical belief that it's wrong to eat animals was going to go down on this hardcore, ultimately practical, home-slaughtering farm. Or, for that matter, how she was going to feel, living in an environment where the fluffy baa-lamb that she was cuddling and bottle-feeding one day would end up as a roast dinner topped by mint sauce the next.

As it turned out, I needn't have worried.

Soon after we arrived at the farm, Joli came to sit beside me on the couch.

'I've decided to start eating meat again,' she said.

'Why's that?' I asked, my mind racing. Had she been feeling pressured? Was it a problem? Had I put her into an unbearable situation?

'Seeing how the animals live here, they have a good life,' she said simply. 'I know they haven't suffered. It just doesn't seem wrong to eat them.'

And that, it appears, was that.

~~~~~~~~~~

After a few months of living happily on the farm, decorating rooms for all the kids and trying to squash my full house of furniture on top of Rich's already full house, Rich asked me to marry him, and I accepted.

We had the ceremony in the dreamily surreal setting of Portmeirion, an Italianate coastal resort in North Wales, with all our friends and family around us done up in Victorian dresses and tail coats. It was the one really perfect day I can remember in my life. The sun was fresh and gold, like the best kind of wine, and we had fireworks on the beach.

For our honeymoon, we decided to go to Provence in southern France. Suddenly the reality of life on a farm caught me up short. You can't just leave. You're meshed into a slowly turning wheel of growing plants and animals that need constant care. We were going away in April, which meant that we had to schedule the lambing to happen *after* we got back. This, in turn, meant the lambs were born late, so they were smaller, so they ate less grass, which affected the hay, which affected the fields in the following year – one small decision, impacting and flowing into areas I'd never imagined.

Suddenly I didn't have to try to wrap my mind around the 'one butterfly flapping its wings can cause a hurricane on the other side of the world' theory. I was living it, every day. Everything on the farm is interconnected to every other thing. And I'm linked into the whole lot, riding the wheel as it slowly turns....

Everything I needed to learn, I realized, could be learned from real things. And from growing our own living food, both plant and animal. I don't remember when it first occurred to me that our food was *alive*. After all, it seems obvious. We are alive, and therefore the food we eat must be alive, to sustain us.

But the food in the supermarket didn't look very alive. Sitting on a shelf, wrapped in plastic, stamped with use-by dates months or even years in the future. As my grandmother used to say, 'If the bugs won't eat it, why should I?'

On the farm, the question of the livingness of food became an issue for me. Over the next few years, I'd become fascinated with living food – the live enzymes and nutrients of our raw goat's milk; the powerful probiotic called kefir that we make from the milk; the way goat's milk penetrates human skin; the mysteries of sourdough starter; the living yeast that makes the bread rise. And following that fascination would lead us down paths that we'd never anticipated.

As farmers, we are, oddly, a little like priests – privileged to stand at the portals where life begins and ends. The seed becomes the sprout, which turns into the tomato plant, under our hands. The sheep quickens with the lamb. We harvest the tomato, and cut it up for our family, and bring it to the table. We eat the lamb. And we're contained irrevocably within its circle – actor and acted upon, bringer of life and death, forever and ever, amen.

~~~~~~~~~~~

2 September 2010

Today I dropped the kids at school, stopped at the feed merchant on the way home and bought one bag of pig food, one bag of beet shreds, two bags of stock mix to feed the goats, and one large container of hypochlorite, the bleach we use to clean the stable and the dairying equipment.

I stood in the drizzling rain while a tall, thin man loaded the heavy bags into my car. I drove home and unloaded them, one by one, laboriously, getting wetter by the minute. They were too heavy for me to lift, so I stacked them onto the sack trolley that Rich had made out of metal bars, and started dragging them up the bumpy, rutted pavement to put them away.

This is exactly the kind of task that I would have had no patience for, long ago in my city life. The kind of job that seems menial and difficult, even pointless. Why perform meaningless drudgery – jobs that strain your muscles and take up your time?

But I've learned a different sort of rhythm on the farm. I know how this one goes – I put on my waterproof coat, my waterproof trousers, my wellies, and go out into the rain. I trudge to the shed and get out the sack trolley. I load the first sack onto it. I pull it up the track. I deliver it. And then I go and get another one.

There's no looking at the watch, no impatient rolling of the eyes, no wondering when this will be finished, or how long it will take. I start into the job with a stolid patience, simply doing what's right in front of me. I'll finish when I finish. And this puts me completely in the moment. No racing ahead – because I can't rush a job like this.

The same goes for hauling in the bales from the hay field – there's no point in standing at the gate, looking over the 200 bales in the hot sun with a sinking heart, wondering how long it'll take. I'll only depress and overwhelm myself.

You have to give yourself to the job, one piece at a time. It has to be done, after all. It must be done. It will be done. And the sweetness – and the acceptance – creeps in from the edges of my mind... peace. The heavy, slow trudging that accomplishes the work also stills and quiets my mind.

This is what I'd lost, as I'd raced faster and faster, turning my work over to machines. The ability to 'give' myself to a task that quiets the mind – and leaves me with a bone-deep, tired sensation of contentment.

'I'm tired – but it's a good tired,' Rich said once, after bringing in the hay. At first I thought he was crazy. How can it be good to be tired? But now I know what he means. It's a different sensation of tiredness than the wired, weary sense of mental exhaustion that comes from racing too fast.

Working hard, deep and slow – I never had this experience before I came to the farm. But it is its own kind of elixir – bitter at first, but soothing and warming in the end. I wouldn't have chosen to drink it, by myself. I did it because I fell in love with Rich – because I wanted to be part of his world, and prove myself strong enough to work beside him; I wanted to be a proper mate, not just a stupid city girl. But having thrown myself into it, I find that the work has its own rewards.

Today, as I trudged through the rain, dragging the heavy trolley, I found myself smiling. In the end, it has everything to do with meaning. I find meaning in what I'm doing, and so I have a serene little separate microclimate in my head of pleasure, despite the mud and the wet.

My work isn't meaningless. It isn't 'dog work'. It means something. The heavy bags are food for the goats – *our* goats. Providing food for the animals, which will provide food for us, stitches me firmly into the wheel of belonging on the farm. My labour isn't random, or empty. It makes me part of a larger whole.

I remember an anecdote about US president John F. Kennedy's visit to the NASA Space Exploration headquarters, during which he stopped to talk to the janitor. 'And what do you do here?' Kennedy asked him kindly. 'I'm helping to put a man on the moon, sir,' the janitor replied. The man wasn't just mopping floors – he was part of something larger.

Human beings, it appears, experience happiness when we feel we're part of something bigger than ourselves. For me, this means being part of the complex and interwoven molecule that is the farm, as intricate and exact as a snowflake. Each piece is connected with every other piece.

I love Rich, and I came to live on the farm with him because this is where he lives. I would have lived on the moon with him, or in the city, or in a tent. But now I'm beginning to love the farm for its own sake – for the things that it's teaching me, and for the life that we live on it.

I'm still travelling for my work – in my other life, I teach high-level executives to give speeches – which I'm beginning to dread. And Rich is still working at the Harp Centre of Wales – but the truth is that he's bored there. He has an engineer's brain along with those fine woodworker's hands, and now that he's helped translate the make-one-harp-a-year process into a more efficient six-harps-a-month, he's doing the same thing over and over, and it doesn't suit him.

I wonder... could we ever make a living from the farm? Is there something here that could make the farm wash its own face? Highly unlikely, I know. From what I can gather it's always a struggle, to make a farm produce income. Usually, you have to farm on a massive scale to make it work economically. But what could we do here, with this lovely little gem of a smallholding overlooking the Irish Sea?

Biofuel, commercial egg-laying, turkeys, Christmas trees? We go to the smallholder shows, and bring back brochures, and talk over the possibilities – we'd love to do something together; something that would mean that neither one of us would have to leave the farm anymore.

14 September 2010

A breezy, blue autumn day – the wind ruffling the curling sycamore leaves and shaking them loose, systematically, from their branches.

It's time to pick blackberries – the hedges around our fields are full of them. This year was supposed to be a good one for these fruits – the combination of frost, sun and rain supposedly created the perfect conditions. But when Rich and I went around the fields last, carrying secateurs to slash back the brambles, some of the blackberries looked wizened and unripe, while others looked already mouldy. We need some sun to ripen them.

Blackberries are one of the great treats of the food year here in Wales. Everyone turns out to pick, filling plastic buckets to the brim, nursing pricked fingers and returning home with berry-stained mouths and clothes. Rich always tempts Benji to eat a sloe, making his whole face shrink up tight with the taste. The tiny sloes, which are unbearably bitter, only come into their own when each one is pricked with a pin (a massive fiddle, when you have hundreds of the things!) and soaked for a year with sugar and gin.

But blackberries are a different thing altogether. I make blackberry and apple jam – apples are due to be picked now as well – and I learned that apples have lots of pectin, the naturally occurring substance that makes jam set. Now I just toss apples into any jam I make – it adds to the flavour, and allows everything to jell perfectly. A secret weapon that I discovered after making many jars of gooey sludge.

33

We're only just now finishing up the final jar from last year. Opening a jar of jam does feel like opening a piece of time that's been bottled – all of our trials and tribulations, laughing and milking, animals dying and being born, bread baking and batches of cheese failing... birthdays and holidays, and the days that stretch in between, all captured in amber like the jam.

We always watch the hedgerows carefully through August, to see when the blackberries are ripe. Welsh tradition says that you should never pick blackberries after 29 September, because that's 'Devil Spits Day', the day that Satan himself is said to spit on all blackberries. No-one seems sure why – one rumour is that, when he was cast out of Heaven, he fell into a bramble patch. Of course, another good reason for not going blackberry picking after that date is that whatever berries have been left by birds and neighbours will most likely be mouldy!

16 September 2010

Yesterday was the day to take our female British Toggenburg, named Marmite, on a date with the local Toggie stud. Goats come into season every 21 days, for a short period in the autumn. After a five-month pregnancy, they give birth in the spring, when the weather is milder, and the grass is growing, ready for the kids to eat.

We don't keep male goats on our farm, because their smell is so horrendous and the males just seem big and scary. So we phoned around to find someone who did keep a proper British Toggenburg gentleman, and would be agreeable to letting it stand stud for us when the time came.

Shann's Blackberry and Apple Jam

675g (1½lb) blackberries

675g (1½lb) apples

150–275ml (¼–½ pint) water

1.3kg (3lb) granulated sugar

1. Pick over the berries and wash them.

2. Peel, core and slice the apples. Put the fruit into a large, heavy-bottomed pan with the water and cook until tender.

3. Add the sugar, and stir until dissolved.

4. Bring to the boil and continue to boil until the jam sets (see below).

5. When the jam has set, pour it into warm, sterilized jars using a ladle or a small pitcher (see below). Seal the jars and allow them to cool.

Don't be intimidated by jam

It's really pretty simple to make jam! You can use any type of fruit that you have to hand, and in any amount. The idea is to boil up fruit with sugar until it's reduced down, and then preserve it in jars.

Really, this is a way of 'preserving' fruit in order to use it over the winter, hence the term 'preserve'. Sugar keeps things from going off — in the same way that salt (brining) or vinegar (pickling) do. These processes are just the ways in which our ancestors dealt with the fact that most of the food on a farm becomes ready at the same time — in the autumn — and needs to be kept so that it can be eaten through the winter, spring and summer.

Many of the classic jam recipes use massive amounts of sugar in order to preserve the fruit. I find this is often too sweet for our taste, so I simply add sugar and taste the mixture until I think it's sweet enough. The downside of this is that the jam may not last as long in the cupboard. But a recipe like this one really only makes between three and four jars of jam, which you'll get through pretty quickly!

A word about 'setting'

I had the worst time, figuring out what this really means! The old country cookbooks assume that every good woman knows all about the technology of making jam — and in my case, it wasn't true. But I finally worked it out, and here's what I discovered: a 'set' means the point at which the jam is cooked enough that it'll be the right consistency to spread on bread once it's cooled.

Here's how to check the 'set point'. Put a saucer in the freezer and let it chill. When you think the jam is cooked enough, put a drop of it on the chilled saucer. Then run your finger through it: if it develops a crinkly track mark when you do so, you have a 'set'.

A word about jars

You don't have to use fancy Kilner jars, although they're lovely if you have the extra cash. Recycled jam jars are fine, as long as they have the plastic-lined lids with the round dot in the middle that 'pops' when they're opened. (All-metal lids will go rusty.)

Place the lids in a pan of boiling water for five minutes and wash the jars carefully. When you start making the jam, set the jars and their lids upside down on a baking tray in a very low oven — about 75°C (175°F). By the time you finish, the jars and lids will be sterilized and warm. This is important, because you need to put the warm jam into warm jars, and seal them. As the jars cool, they'll compress, creating a seal that will pull that lid down tight. When you open it, you should hear the 'pop'.

And a final note on pectin

This is a great recipe because it has apples in it, and as I've learned, apples have pectin — the stuff that makes jam set. You can buy preserving sugar that has added pectin, but I find it simpler just to chuck two or three apples into whatever I'm making. They don't disturb the flavour or texture, and do ensure that your jam will be a good consistency — not too runny. So, throw in some apples!

Enjoy! There's nothing more heavenly than homemade jam on homemade bread — everyone will crowd round the kitchen table.

We'd marked on the calendar the first day that Marmite came into season, and then carefully counted ahead 21 days, and marked it again. Yesterday there was no sign of anything different about her, but when I went out to milk this morning she was bleating and wagging her tail – definitely in season. Nothing noisier than a female goat in the mood for love!

I sighed – I'd been hoping that she'd wait until Rich got home. I phoned him at work and he said that I could wait until he returned at 2:30 p.m., but I was worried that it'd be too late – sometimes goats only stay in season for a few hours.

On my own, then. I hooked up the new trailer – purchased specially for this purpose, and small enough for me to tow legally – nerves jangling and stomach tight. I went over and over in my head what Rich had told me – click the latch of the hitch down firmly in place, loop the chain over the round ball, plug in the lights, wind the extra wheel up out of the way and clamp it down. I'd never towed anything on my own before... just one practice run with Rich beside me in the passenger seat.

It's a funny thing, as I had all kinds of adventures in my days of newspaper and radio. I went undercover into *Playboy* founder Hugh Hefner's wedding... sneaked into a Moonie brainwashing encampment for a weekend... pretended to be a high school senior for a month to write a story on the education system in California.

I'd brashly agreed to take on a radio show with no previous experience, and bluffed my way through many an interview and live stage show, facing an audience of thousands. But nothing I've ever done reduces me to the helpless, quivering pile of nerves that I feel when confronted with farm machinery.

Big, blunt and fiercely coloured, it seems particularly unforgiving. It appears to leer at me threateningly, warning me that it could take off an arm or a leg, or hurt someone I love, if I don't know what I'm doing. And let's face it – I don't.

Before when I didn't know what I was doing, I was always able to fake it. I specialized in being a 'just-add-water' kind of expert. Jump off the cliff and figure it out on the way down was my motto. In the city, a big attitude and a breezy line of chatter will take you a long way. I often waited until the hour before my radio show to prepare, counting on my ability to skim the material quickly, and make it all work at show time.

I liked the challenge. But this is real life, real stuff. You have to actually know what you're doing, or animals will die, tractors will overturn, dumpers will get stuck in the mud. You can't fake it, and that terrifies me.

I checked to see that there was enough straw in the back of the trailer to make a comfortable bed, and went to get Marmite. She seemed happy enough to come along and leaped nimbly into the trailer. I bolted her in, and we set off on our journey.

I had the postcode of the location of the stud goat, and I typed it into the sat nav. We drove along for 30 minutes or so. I was taking particular care to start and stop smoothly, so as not to jolt Marmite. I was feeling pretty proud of myself.

Then the sat nav told me to turn left, and I did, only to find myself trapped in a residential cul-de-sac. Obviously not the farm that I'd been heading for – and no room to turn around.

For nearly 10 minutes I tried fruitlessly to back out. But with the trailer behind me swinging immediately right or left, there was no way I could do it. I tried to back the trailer into a driveway – no luck. By then I was sweating and shaking and near to tears, and Marmite was bleating piteously in the back.

Eventually, I got out of the car, unhooked the trailer, turned the car around, dragged the trailer back into position by hand, hooked it up again, and drove out.

Back on the road, I passed several farm lanes that roughly matched the description the woman had given me, but I was too frightened to drive down them, in case they were the wrong ones, and I was unable to get back out again. I phoned the billy owner, and she didn't pick up the phone. I phoned Rich, and he was sympathetic, but there wasn't a lot he could do. I was just going to have to sort this out myself.

Finally, after passing one stone church at least three times, stopping to ask kindly but ultimately unhelpful men in a nearby village and banging my forehead on the steering wheel repeatedly, I managed to reach the billy lady on the phone, and she directed me to the correct farm track. We bumped along a narrow dirt road for nearly a mile before she came out to greet us, smiling and waving.

She was kindly, with wild brown curly hair, not unlike my own – and jeans tucked into her wellies. I recognized her as a kindred spirit at once. People who keep goats nearly always have wild hair. I think it has something to do with always being out in the barn, and having bits of straw fall on you all the time.

She showed me the two male goats she kept – a handsome silver one with a beard, and a younger, slighter one who was a darker brown. The smell of the billies enveloped us, eye-wateringly strong, musky and almost – but not quite – like pine resin. She asked me which one I'd prefer. Ooh, a difficult question, and another of those things that I would've referred to Rich if only he'd been with me.

Marmite is quite a light Toggenburg, and they're really supposed to be darker, in order to win prizes at shows. We don't show our goats at the moment, but we might choose to next year. This would mean a vote for the darker male. But the lighter male had a slightly better-looking pedigree, as his dam's milk yields had been recorded. This gives the all-important 'Q*' rating next to the name on the pedigree – a mark of goat-y success.

This was another entirely new world for me. I've never been an enthusiastic breeder of any sort of animal, and the goat world has as many tricky ins and outs, arcane references and incomprehensible expert jargon as any private arena can. I now find myself knee-deep in this obsession, to the point where Rich and I are both proud possessors of 'South West Wales Goat Club' patches, ready to be sewn onto our jackets. Sad, really.

The goat world also seems to have an incredible amount of complicated paperwork, involving registering and transferring the animals back and forth between owners. Each time they are born, or die, or are sold, or move from one place to another, blue and green and pink copies of forms have to be filled out, ripped off, mailed or filed. I wrestle with this paperwork, and with the mysterious codes next to the names of really 'good' animals that indicate breeding or milk yield or something. It's all very confusing.

In the end, I plumped for the lighter male, simply because I liked the way he looked. He was grand and handsome, with intelligent eyes and a silvery beard – he reminded me a bit of Rich, if I'm honest.

I thought I'd delicately duck out and give Marmite some private time with her beau – I didn't quite know how this bit of it was handled. No such luck. I was instructed to hold Marmite while the male came out of his shed, jumped up on top of her and heaved away for a few seconds. And then, apparently, it was all over. Marmite looked as stunned as I felt.

We tied her up, away from the male goat, and went into a little caravan parked in the barnyard to do the paperwork. I wrote out a cheque, and the lady handed me the carefully printed pedigree of the male I'd chosen to act as stud. Then we went outside again, repeated the whole process – with me holding Marmite still while the male covered her a second time – just to make sure, and then we were finished.

I loaded Marmite back into the trailer, and we drove home, covered in glory and billy stench. And Rich welcomed me home with open arms and told me that he was proud of me. I had to wash my hair twice to get out all the billy odour, and even my handbag smelled for days afterwards.

20 September 2010

Every Friday night we go out for fish and chips. Everyone who happens to be home piles into several cars and we drive for 15 minutes to reach St Dogmaels – a charming little seaside town that flings its pink, yellow and blue cottages over hills sloping down to the sea. St Dogmaels is famous for two things – Bowen's Fish and Chip Shop, which is without a doubt the best fish and chip shop in West Wales, and its mermaid legend, sworn to be true by the people who live there. The story goes like this:

There was once a fisherman named Peregrine, who lived in a terraced cottage at Cwmmins, St Dogmaels. Peregrine was out fishing one day at Cemaes Head, casting his nets for herring, when he pulled up a mermaid instead. She begged to be put back into the sea, but Peregrine would have none of it. He tied her up firmly and headed back for land.

But as he sailed, the mermaid wept and sobbed so piteously that he finally gave in, and released her back into the sea, near the bar at the estuary.
Before she swam away, the grateful mermaid promised to tell Peregrine whenever there was a storm approaching.

On 30 September 1789, Peregrine and many other fishermen set out for a day's fishing. The sky looked fine and clear. But when Peregrine's boat reached the bar, he saw the head of his mermaid emerge. She warned him that there would be a terrible storm that day. He heeded her warning and turned back, trying to persuade the other fishermen to return to St Dogmaels with him. They just laughed at him and carried on out to sea.

Suddenly, the southwest wind veered around to the northwest and blew a sort of hurricane. A terrible storm followed, and the sea ran as high as a mountain, carrying everything before it. The fishing boats were smashed like twigs; some thrown onto the beach, others onto rocks. All the fishermen perished – except Peregrine and his crew.

This story is memorialized by a statue of the mermaid, looking wistfully out towards the bar at the mouth of the River Teifi. I've often looked at this figure, smooth and sinuous in wood, with her strange, pensive expression, and thought about the tale. It's so perfectly Welsh in its specificity, its strange blend of matter-of-fact mystery and pragmatism.

In a classic fairy tale, there might be a romance between Peregrine and the mermaid, and some grand conclusion. But in the Welsh story, Peregrine and the mermaid strike quite a mundane bargain – she tells him about the storm. No palace, no marriage, no gold ring, no nonsense – just a sensible weather warning, which he sensibly accepts. And the naming of dates and locations is so exact – the story even gives Peregrine's address.

Wales is a place so steeped in magic that each location has its own fairy tale, and there's a shoulder-shrugging acceptance of obvious things like mermaids and dragons. It's said that the last dragon in Wales was killed in Newcastle Emlyn, just down the road from us, and the story even reports that the river was polluted for two weeks afterwards.

In any case, Bowen's Fish and Chip Shop is real and warm, and we greet it gratefully each Friday evening, driving up the long hill and looking eagerly to see whether it's open. We know it's open, of course, because we always phone ahead. But we look anyway.

The restaurant and takeaway are run by Mr and Mrs Bowen, an irrepressibly cheerful couple who always manage to smile, despite their gruelling schedule. Mr Bowen gets up at 6 a.m. to cut up all the potatoes for chips, and the two of them cook and serve all the food until night. In the summer, when the tourists come, they hire a lovely lady with bright pink hair to help at the counter.

The place is always immaculate, hung with black-and-white photos of St Dogmaels in decades gone by. The fish is fresh, the batter delicious and crunchy and never greasy. We always order the same things… and Mrs Bowen always remembers our order, so that we can just ask for 'our regular'.

The Bowens are very attached to Benji, who at four-and-a-half has a round, cherubic face and a cowslick sticking his hair straight up on one side. They gave him a watch once, which he wears proudly, although he can't yet tell the time. And they ply him with sweets, and let him hand round the container of lollipops which gets offered to customers after their meal. Last time we went, Benji went into the kitchen and offered Mrs Bowen a kiss, much to her amusement.

Once, after we'd left the restaurant, I commented on the Bowens' kindness to Benji, trying to work it out.

'It has to do with *perthyn*,' Rich said.

'What?' I asked.

'*Perthyn*.' He thought for a minute. 'There's not really an English translation for it. It has to do with a connection. It means "related to", but it also means belonging.'

45

Perthyn. I asked him to write it down for me, so I could think about it later. Every once in a while I come across a Welsh word that has no equivalent in English. Welsh is a misty, romantic language, with soft edges. It has no harsh swear words of its own, and when Welsh people want to talk about hard-edged things like money or science, or when they want to swear, they usually slip back into English. But there are complicated, delicate concepts that can only be expressed in Welsh.

Not only is there no translation for *perthyn* in English, but I'd never even considered such a thing. Connection, relation, belonging. Ties.

If there were one way that my life before could be described, it would be by its complete lack of *perthyn*. I was an only child, and my parents took me away from our extended family in Texas when I was very young. We floated in a rare and isolated bubble, my parents and I, just the three of us.

We were always strangers in our neighbourhood in some sense, even when we'd lived there for many years. When the time came, we casually sold all of our belongings in a yard sale, and moved across the entire country to start again in California. And when the time came again, I left even my parents behind and crossed the ocean to go to a new country.

Perthyn is not something that I ever learned, or experienced, or felt before. But now, it seems that I've found it at last.

The leaves are dropping, and the wind is beginning to bite. We're doing all the things around the farm that Rich calls 'battening down the hatches' for the winter. Preparing for the coming rains, he's dug a gutter under the sill of his new shed, and lined it neatly with concrete so the water runs into a mesh-covered pipe in the centre. Benji watches the water running in this with great fascination, and religiously keeps the leaves swept out so that it runs properly.

Benji and Rich together closed off the end of the shed with reclaimed sheets of tin and posts from the barn, and have started shifting all the firewood logs to this new location, closer to the path and easier to reach from the house. They took the quad bike down to the woods last weekend and came back up with heavy rounds of oak, which Rich has been steadily sawing into chunks.

This wood won't be ready for burning for another two years, but to miss out a year of wood gathering means there'll be a hole in the cycle when the time comes. We had the first fire of the year in the wood burner the other night, and the dry, radiant heat spread through the room like butter over toast. We all sighed and snuggled into the leather sofa, smelled the wood smoke and counted ourselves lucky.

I've been thinking about this *perthyn* thing that Rich keeps talking about. *Perthyn* – connection, relationship. Here on the farm, everything is about *perthyn*.

Rich's father, Taid, lives in an apartment connected to the house. He has his own kitchen, lounge, bedroom, porch and garden, but he joins us for supper each night. He's independent when he wants to be, but surrounded by people when he chooses. When we bale the straw, Taid comes out with a wooden rake to rake up the bits that are left behind, and put them into bags, because he no longer has the massive strength needed to lift the bales and swing them onto the trailer. But at age 72, he's still part of the farm. That's *perthyn.*

And someday, Benji will lift the bales, and it'll be Rich who rakes up the bits left behind. It'll be Rich and I, maybe, who live in the little apartment at the back, and our children and their children who live in the big farmhouse. That, too, is *perthyn.*

And in the end, *perthyn* even applies to our food. We have a relationship with it. For example, we recently bought in some bull calves, to be turned into beef, for our roast dinners. But at the moment, they are babies. We teach our dinner to drink milk, and it looks back at us with wide, round eyes. I resist this massive sense of connection, because it feels painful. The heartstrings that tie everything together tug and pull in my chest.

I'm more accustomed to indifference – to the anonymity of the city, and distance. Floating in isolation is peaceful. To live in this awakened net of connections means that every change, every fluctuation, has its answer in a flickering nerve ending of my own. I'm connected to people and animals and growing things, and each time one of them grows or dies or changes, it affects me – and sometimes it hurts. The fairy tale of connection sounds wonderful, but the reality can be painful, like a frostbitten limb coming back to life. I hadn't thought of that.

I want to get some sourdough bread starter.

I'm not sure why. In a way, it's an unlikely thing to do. As far as I know, sourdough is a pioneer tradition from the USA, and it's not something that the Welsh people are really familiar with. When I asked him about sourdough, Rich just looked at me blankly.

But I've this little idea that keeps niggling at me: to get some sourdough starter. I've a picture in the back of my mind of a pioneer woman in a covered wagon, setting out for the new world, a calico poke bonnet on her bowed head and a wooden bowl containing sourdough starter on her knees. That sourdough is her security – her insurance. No matter what happens on the long, unimaginable road to the place she doesn't yet know, she'll be able to make bread for her family. As long as she has her sourdough, she can feed the people she loves.

I suppose I've done just the opposite – I've left the new world, to come back to the old. Maybe I too want some sourdough as insurance for my journey.

The thing about sourdough is that it's lineage food. You can take a little bit of it, and make your bread. Save some back, and it'll make another batch. You can keep it indefinitely, passing it down from generation to generation, keeping it alive. A little bit of the old world, alive in the new.

In Ireland, apparently, they have the same idea with kefir, a fermented milk product that's like yogurt. My Irish friend Barbara told me that in Ireland the woman of the house is the steward of the kefir, which is valued for its health-giving properties.

As with sourdough, you can hold back a bit of kefir and start a new batch with it, so it can be kept going forever. When a son marries, his mother gives a bit of the family kefir to his new wife, thus passing on the responsibility for his health and wellbeing. What a lovely idea. Hmmm... can I get some kefir grains? How does it work? Where can I buy them? Must remember to look it up.

I love this idea – the woman as the holder of the family's health, using food with history to nourish. Food that has tradition, and meaning. Curious as to what's behind this circling sourdough thought that keeps nudging at me, I look it up online. I'm ravished by the images that come up.

Sourdough, which is believed to be more healthful than other types of bread because of the fermentation process that makes it sour, has been used since biblical times. And sourdough is sexy. Legend has it that sourdough bread became popular because of the belief that baking powder was an anti-aphrodisiac. Men who feared losing their virility by eating biscuits made with baking powder chose sourdough bread instead.

Families and bakeries throughout the world own sourdough starters that are many human generations old, revered for creating a special taste or texture. The practice of making and baking sourdough is steeped in tradition and ritual. For thousands of years, in each village, the peasant women of Europe all baked on the same day, so that they could use the communal stone bread ovens.

Each woman would take her starter, saved from the previous week's dough, and mix it with new ingredients. The dough was left to rise – with a piece held back, to be the starter for the following week. The rest was formed into loaves that were marked with the family sign, the source of the traditional slashing of bread loaves. The bread was then taken to the village ovens to bake.

The individual, braided seamlessly into the communal. Each family with its own distinct mark – but all the loaves in the same oven. Unique, but connected.

I can imagine the fires being lit in the great ovens, the creaking wooden doors, the stones glowing red-hot, the loaves being shovelled in – each with a different sign cut into the crust – the perfume of the baking bread, the women leaning on fences and gossiping before gathering to collect their loaves and take them home... I can almost smell the bread.

I read on and learned that you can use sourdough to make cookies, cakes and waffles – or to tan a hide, cure an aching back, as a glue for sealing a letter or a paste to paper a cabin. So many uses.

I also found something that I should have remembered – that sourdough was the main bread made in Northern California during the California Gold Rush of the late 19th century, and has remained a major part of the culture of San Francisco. The bread was so common that 'sourdough' became a general nickname for the gold prospectors.

I came to Wales from Northern California, and San Francisco is as close to an original home for me as anything can be. So the thought of bringing a piece of my heritage to Wales, and braiding it into the food traditions that we follow here, seems right and lovely. A little bit of the new world, here in the old. Food for my journey... food for my thoughts.

There's also something else that I like about sourdough, and kefir – something that has to do with its ability to reproduce itself, and maintain a lineage through time. I suppose it has to do with aliveness.

These things are alive – actual microorganisms that live and create a certain effect. They ferment the milk, or make the bread rise. They need certain things to survive, and neglect – or too much salt – will kill them. By feeding the sourdough starter, or the kefir, we're interacting with the tiny organisms that we can't see.

It's like our bull calves, but on the tiniest cellular level. We feed the calves, and the calves feed us. We feed the sourdough, and the sourdough feeds us. A closed circuit of interaction, like touching two wires together and feeling power flow. A relationship.

Maybe that's it – I can't have a relationship with a plastic-wrapped container of yogurt, or a loaf of bread that I buy from the shop. It's a dead end. It doesn't mean anything. I throw away the wrapping and eat the product. That's all there is to it.

But the kefir, or the sourdough – there's a whole world of mystery contained there. It has its story, its legends, its thousands of years of history. I can touch that history, and blend it into my own family's history.

As I use my hands to make the bread that will feed my family, I can tell myself the stories and the images linger in my mind – the women by the stone ovens, the gold prospectors by the fireside, the pioneer woman in her poke bonnet, clutching her wooden bowl. The tiny living organisms in the bowl as I stir it are like a universe in reverse, as small as the stars are distant, world upon world.

In a wonderful crystallization of this heritage, Joli has now picked up the torch to carry it forward, playing with the marvellous idea of creating a healing 'medical bread' that's actually good for you.

She's frequently to be found in the farmhouse kitchen up to her elbows in flour, making up recipes, kneading dough and experimenting with new ways to ferment starter. Here's what Joli has to say about bread:

'I love bread. The history and mystery, the crusts and shapes, grains and textures. How have we managed to make something so necessary and magical into such a pointless, empty food? It frustrates me to hear things like, "wheat is bad, don't eat bread", because bread is in almost every culture, so we simply can't be doing it right.

'There's a right way to cook wheat so that it doesn't make you sick: sourdough. Bread made with a sourdough or leaven (starter) is a fermented food and it's the oldest way to create your daily loaf. Sure, it takes time, but it's not your time.

'I use rye flour in my sourdough because it's low in gluten, highly nutritious, high in wild yeasts (making it very easy and quick to get your starter active) and you can use it to raise loaves made with flours from other grains, such as wheat and spelt. My favourite would have to be an all-rye sourdough. The best bread book I ever found was Andrew Whitley's *Bread Matters*. It's a beautiful book about a beautiful subject.'

1 October 2010

Chucking with rain today, the sky covered with an austere white fog. It's gone cold – feeling more like winter all the time. I took the children to school this morning, came back and gratefully crawled back into bed, curling up against Rich's warm back – he had the day off from work. He got up to milk the goats later, and brought me back a cup of tea. I drank it propped up in bed, looking out at the misty mountain that stretches outside the window, just before the sea.

We're continuing to do things that mark the onset of the cold season – including arranging to sweep out the chimney of the wood burner. For kindling, we burn the scraps of wood that Rich brings home from his work as a harp maker. For the bigger logs, we have stocks that Rich has cut from our woodlands, at the bottom of the sloping fields.

The woodlands lurk at the edge of the farm, full of mystery, and plants that the goats like to nibble. On a fine day, when we let them out of their stalls after feeding and milking them, our little herd will bound down the hill, jumping and bouncing sideways, and disappear as a group into the woods.

Goats are really browsers, not grazers – they prefer to eat leaves, and bark, and pieces of even the sharpest and most inhospitable trees – holly and gorse. Amazing that their mouths are so soft, and yet they can ingest things that I can't handle without gloves.

Joli's Rye Sourdough Bread

Prepare the starter

1. Mix 50g (2oz) rye flour with 25ml (1 fl oz) lukewarm water in a breathable (not glass) container — e.g. a Tupperware box, or a bowl covered with clingfilm — the gases produced in the fermentation process can break your container.

2. Continue to add 50g (2oz) rye flour and 25ml (1 fl oz) lukewarm water every day for a minimum of four days, by which point your sour should be bubbly on top and smelling... sour! You can now use this 'starter' to make bread whenever you want — it's active! Don't worry if there is some separation.

Make the 'production sourdough'

1. Mix 50g (2oz) of the starter with 150g (5oz) rye flour and 300ml (10 fl oz) lukewarm water.

2. With wet hands, place the dough in a bowl, cover and leave until the next morning/ evening, depending on when you started. This is your 'production sourdough'.

Make the sourdough bread

1. Make your final dough with 450g (1lb) of your production sourdough (tip the rest back into your starter), 350g (12oz) rye flour, 2 tsp salt and 200ml (7 fl oz) lukewarm water. This dough should be very wet, and you don't need to knead it, given that rye flour is so low in gluten.

2. Leave the dough to rise until the next morning/evening and then bake for up to an hour at 200°C (400°F). It's better to let the loaf sit for a day before cutting into it. Don't be alarmed by the flat top.

This bread is a gift to yourself, your family, and your health. Find a way for it to fit into your routine unobtrusively, so that it can bring you pleasure instead of extra stress.

~~~~~~~~~~~~~~~~~~~~~

It's a strange thing with the goat's cheese. For a while, I was turning out successful batch after successful batch. It was great. People were buying it (well, giving me donations in exchange for it). Just friends, and people around the office. It was pretty good stuff.

And then – bang. Suddenly the batches started going wrong, and I haven't been able to make a successful batch since. I altered everything I could think of – bought new rennet, made a new batch of starter. Nothing. Instead of a dense, grainy texture, the cheese would be too fluffy, or rubbery, with strange holes. I've pored through my books without any luck. Now I wonder if I'm actually the worst cheese maker in the world.

And the really sad thing is, I keep trying. Batch after batch. I fail each time, and miserably pour the results into the pig bucket. I'm not sure why I don't give up. I've got a batch sitting on the table now. I should go and turn it, but I can't bear to see what I'm bound to see when I do.

I'll have to phone Margaret Grant, the doyenne of the goat club. She and her husband Ian have been keeping goats for 40 years, and she's been making cheese for most of that time. We bought our beautiful white British Saanen goat, Glenda the Good (herd name Kattern Gwenlan), from the Grants, and what the Grants don't know about goats and goat's cheese isn't worth knowing. I'll ask them to come round and tell me what I'm doing wrong.

4 October 2010

Since I'm doing so poorly with my cheese making as a way to use the goat's milk, I thought I'd turn my attention back to goat's milk kefir. I've learned that kefir is a fermented milk that's very like yogurt, but with a stronger probiotic effect. Yogurt has 'transient' bacteria that only help you while they're in your digestive system – they get killed off by the digestive process, so you have to keep eating it. Kefir, on the other hand, is so powerful that it actually permanently repopulates your gut with good flora and fauna.

All I know is that goat's milk kefir makes brilliant smoothies, and that Benji is never happier than when he's blending up frozen fruit and bananas and homemade goat's milk kefir into a milk shake.

After finding such interesting information about sourdough starter online, I thought I'd look up the history of kefir. Apparently it's one of the oldest cultured milk products in existence, originating in the Caucasus Mountains in Eurasia.

Kefir grains are mysterious little white things that look a bit like small cauliflowers. They're not actual grains, like wheat grains, but instead small colonies of microbiotics – beneficial yeasts and bacteria. They are living, and actually grow and multiply, so if you have a batch, it'll soon grow large enough that you can divide it and give some to a friend.

Oddly, no-one seems to know where the first kefir grain came from. But what we do know is that when you put kefir grains into milk, and leave it to ferment over 48 hours at room temperature, the resulting drink – similar to buttermilk in taste and consistency – is one of the most powerful probiotics available.

The people who live on the northern slopes of the Caucasus Mountains say that Muhammad gave kefir grains to the Orthodox people, and taught them how to make kefir. These 'Grains of the Prophet' were jealously guarded, since it was believed that they would lose their strength if they were given away and the secret of how to use them became common knowledge.

Traditionally, kefir was made from cow's or goat's milk, in animal-hide sacks. The kefir sacks were hung in the sun during the day, and brought back into the house at night, where they were hung by the door. Everyone who entered or left the house was expected to prod the sack with their foot to mix the contents. As kefir was removed, more fresh milk was added, making the fermentation process continuous.

Kefir grains were considered part of the wealth of family and tribe, something to be cherished and passed on from generation to generation. So for centuries the people of the northern Caucasus hoarded their kefir and cultivated it, without sharing it with outsiders. Other people occasionally heard strange tales of this unusual beverage, which was said to have magical properties; Marco Polo mentions kefir in the chronicles of his travels in the East. But for centuries, kefir was largely forgotten outside the Caucasus.

Until news spread of its use in sanatoria for the treatment of tuberculosis, and its efficacy in the healing of intestinal and stomach diseases. Russian doctors believed that kefir was beneficial for health, and the first scientific studies were published at the end of the 19th century. But scientific investigation was hampered by the fact that kefir was so difficult to obtain. Commercial production simply wasn't possible, without first obtaining a source of the grains.

The members of the All Russian Physician's Society were determined to find a source for the kefir grains – in order to make kefir available to their patients – so they sent a beautiful young woman named Irina Sakharova to the court of a Caucasian prince, Bek-Mirza Barchorov. Irina was instructed to charm the prince, and persuade him to give her some of the kefir grains. The prince was very taken with Irina, but his fear of retribution for violating religious law was stronger than his lust – he refused to give her any of the 'Grains of the Prophet'.

Realizing that their mission had failed, Irina and her party departed for the Russian spa city of Kislovodsk. But halfway home, they were taken captive by armed mountain tribesmen, who seized Irina and took her back to Prince Bek-Mirza Barchorov. It was a local custom to steal a bride – and Irina was told to prepare to marry the prince.

The Russian government mounted a daring rescue mission and saved Irina from her forced marriage just in time. The matter was brought in front of the Tsar, who ruled that the prince must give Irina 4.5kg (10lb) of the precious grains in recompense for the insults she'd endured.

The kefir grains were taken in triumph to the Moscow Dairy, and in September 1908, the first bottles of kefir drink were offered for sale in Moscow. Commercial manufacture of kefir began on a large scale in Russia in the 1930s. And in 1973 the minister of the food industry of the Soviet Union sent a letter to Irina Sakharova, now an old woman, to thank her for bringing kefir to the Russian people.

Today kefir is the most popular fermented milk drink in Russia – the Russians consume an average of 4.5kg (10lb) of it per person, per year. Kefir is also made on a commercial scale in the Czech Republic, Finland, Hungary, Norway, Poland, Sweden, Switzerland, some of the former Soviet Union states, Denmark, the USA, France, Germany, Canada and parts of Southeast Asia. It's been used to help IBS, eczema, allergies, acne, and auto-immune disorders, and some researchers have even tested it against tumours.

And to think that I have a bottle of the grains in my refrigerator right now! I was able to order some online. They came in a tiny plastic packet – but quickly doubled and then doubled again as I used them.

How to Make Drinking Kefir

I packet of kefir grains (luckily for us, these are now easily available online!)

I litre (1¾ pints) of fresh milk (we use raw goat's milk, but any type will do).

1. Put the kefir grains in a clean I-litre (1¾-pint) container with a lid (a Kilner jar is perfect) and cover them with the milk. Don't use a metal container, and be careful with plastic, because the kefir is acidic (the plastic tubs used for yogurt are fine).

2. Sit at room temperature for 8–12 hours. More if you'd prefer a stronger, fizzier or thicker kefir. The kefir may separate. That's okay — just shake it up!

3. Strain the grains out of the mixture with a plastic (not metal) strainer. The resultant strained liquid is your drinking kefir.

4. Then rinse the kefir grains with some fresh milk, and return them to a clean container. Cover with milk again. Remember that your kefir is a living thing. Properly cared for, it will live as long as you do.

5. Feed it milk to keep it alive. If it uses up all the available milk, it'll starve. If you go away or don't need your kefir

for a while, put it in the fridge, where it'll go to sleep!
When you're ready for it again, simply put it back on the
kitchen worktop at room temperature.

In its unflavoured state, kefir is quite acidic — like a fizzy
natural yogurt. We like to blend it up with ripe bananas,
vanilla, organic sugar and avocado for a super-smoothie.
Don't use honey to sweeten it, though — as honey is
naturally antibiotic it will interfere with the probiotics in
the kefir.

7 October 2010

A nondescript, greyish day today. Not really cold enough to
justify making a morning fire, and not wet enough to skulk
inside. The day before yesterday it was nearly icy, and I did
make a fire in the wood burner, and then did my stretches in
front of it, luxuriating in the heat. I kept the fire going for much
of the morning, periodically feeding pieces of wood into the
heavy black metal stove.

As I pulled the kindling out of the feed sack, it struck me how
similar this process is to the others I have going at the moment:

feed wood into the fire; strain the kefir grains out of the goat's milk kefir, and feed it fresh milk; water the herbs that I've started, from cuttings taken from other herbs. And when I make my sourdough starter, which I'm hoping to do today, I'll be feeding the starter with fresh flour and water, to keep it going.

All these things – the kefir, the starter, the herbs – replicate themselves, as only living things can do. Once started, they can recreate themselves indefinitely, given some care. They're linked in a cycle of perpetual growth and rebirth – and they link me into that cycle, as well.

It's Rich's *perthyn* again, I think, but on a whole different level. We've been talking about *perthyn* as it applies to family, and to a community. This is *perthyn* on a microscopic level, with the tiny living organisms that ferment the goat's milk kefir and leaven the bread. They are alive, so they need to feed. And you can only have a relationship with things that are alive.

Maybe it comes down to that, in the end. I want my food to be alive – and I want to have a relationship with it. I feed my food, before it feeds me.

We often wonder what we're doing here, trying to be self-sufficient. After all, we'll never truly be 'off the grid' – we use electricity, and computers, and diesel for the cars and tractors. We don't come close to producing all of our own fruit and vegetables. And even the things that I can make – bread, jam, cheese (well, sort of!) – I don't make all the time.

Shop-bought bread is easier for sandwiches. Cheddar cheese melts better than goat's cheese. And so we buy the things that we need. The things that we make for ourselves are almost extra – luxury items.

But I think, for me, it's not about trying to pull away from society or save money. I simply want more of a quality of aliveness in my life.

Sure, I can buy tomatoes wrapped in plastic from the shop. But when I plant a tomato seed, feed it with compost from our sheep, water it with water from our spring, pinch out the side shoots, watch over it and talk to it and rejoice when it flowers, wait for the small green fruit to ripen, and finally, after many weeks, with infinite satisfaction, twist it gently off the stem – that's not a tomato; that's a relationship. It's a real and enduring passion, as real as any love affair. Put it in your mouth and bite down on the sweet, explosive burst of tomato-ness – that's not food. That's a feast.

20 October 2010

I went away to Amsterdam for work, and when I returned something terrible happened. I'm not even sure what it was.

I work with an old comrade and friend from California, who kindly rescued me and gave me a job after I walked out on my abusive ex-husband, with my two small children in tow. I was, at the time, homeless and unemployed and stranded in a strange country. The lifeline that Peter threw me was the one thing that enabled me to survive and support my kids. I was desperately grateful to him.

Peter's company, Stand & Deliver, is based in California, and he sends teams of trainers all over the world to do lightning-fast presentation trainings. We work in two- or three-day chunks, once a month, flying into an airport, going directly to a hotel, working 12-hour days and then flying home.

The work is interesting, adrenaline-charged and completely intellectual, and a million miles from the slow, steady warmth of the farm. The rooms where I work are illuminated by over-bright lights, the hotels luxurious but strangely sterile, and the airports marvels of arid plastic and steel.

I love what I do, although this time I was more riddled with guilt than usual at leaving my family and the farm. It's too much to leave on Rich's shoulders – the double school run, his own work, the animals to be fed and milked twice a day, the shopping, the cooking. It's a two-person gig, and, for me to bow out for an entire week and leave him on his own with it seems horribly unfair.

But we needed the money. The farm, with all its rich resonance, doesn't produce an income, and feeding 11 goats, two calves, two pigs and 24 sheep doesn't come cheap. So after much discussion, we agreed that I would do the job.

I was gone for five days. I worked hard and well – successfully coaching some executives – fell into bed exhausted at the end of the overstimulating days, and then returned. There were welcome-home banners on the windows of the farmhouse, and I handed out the duty-free chocolates I'd bought at the airport. It should have all been fine.

But something was wrong. For days after I came home, I felt crippled by the most overwhelming despair. Suddenly, nothing meant anything.

I remembered all the projects that had engaged me so completely – the sourdough, the yogurt, the goat's milk kefir – and I couldn't remember why it was worth bothering with them. I was tired, surely? But it was more than that – it felt as if everything was too much trouble, like there was no point. I couldn't find a way back *in*.

It was as if some corrosive acid had been poured over thousands of small and fragile root tendrils that were creeping their way across a wall, linking things together. And all the root filaments had shrivelled, disappeared. My tiny farm projects were no match for the devastating cold of the outside world, with its weight of ambition, speed and lethal competition.

Who cared about sourdough? There were careers to be made, battles to be fought and won – and it's difficult to argue the merits of goat's milk kefir with someone who has to give a presentation to the CEO the next day.

It might have been hormones – it might have been fatigue. All I knew is that when I left, the room of my life was warm and brightly lit – and when I came back, it was as if the lights had been turned out. Same room, but all dark.

I fought down the edges of panic and carried on. Slept as much as I could, waiting for the flavour and savour of life to return. Did the rounds, fed the animals, marked the calendar, trudged through the school run.

The to-do list was frightening – all the things that had been undone while I was away, plus the expenses and summation and invoice that needed to be generated for the work trip just completed. A book deal was falling apart. My parents wanted to take one grandchild on holiday, and leave the other three at home. Everywhere I turned, everything seemed like the most impossible mess.

Yesterday, I got up knowing that I had a million things to do. Taid's birthday is coming up – we're planning to have the entire family round on Saturday. Gifts had to be purchased and a meal planned. An urgent work assignment needed completing.

But first, I had to feed and milk the animals. And unlike executives, there's no negotiating with animals. Sighing, I pushed my unwilling feet into my wellies, pulled on my waterproof trousers and trudged outside.

The sunlight was dappling the rough grey stone of the building across the farmyard from the house. Water poured from the mouth of the stone lion fountain. There was an edge to the breeze, and two red-tailed kites, among those carefully nurtured back from the edge of extinction, soared and dipped over the muted blue of the sea.

I tipped a pail of vegetable peelings into the pig's trough, topped it up with pig pellets, and filled the other end with water. The pigs rooted through the vegetables happily, grunting and squealing. Their pleasure made me smile in spite of myself.

I carried on into the barn, passing the ranks of familiar, beloved goat faces. The two Anglo-Nubian pedigree princesses, Conkers and Seren, lay regally at the back of their stall and looked disapproving. Lola, stroppy but glistening, leaned on the wall like a dance-hall floozy in a saloon, demanding a scratch behind the ears. Athletic little Toffee hurled herself against the reinforced bars of her stall, trying to jump out. And placid Glenda gazed out with the assurance of a queen bee, waiting to be milked.

I talked to them and turned on the radio while I fed the calves their milk, watching them root around in the buckets to suck out the last drops. Pulling hay out of the stack, I looked straight down into the eyes of a tiny black kitten, crouching, spitting and snarling behind the hay. We have a community of barn cats who live with us in dignified symbiosis – we feed them, and they keep the rats away, but they aren't pets. We don't generally handle them, unless they're ill or injured.

This one, though, I reached down and picked up so that it wouldn't get crushed by the hay. I stroked it until it calmed down, rubbing it behind the ear until it began to purr; finally, it lay relaxed and contented in my hands. And then, for some reason, I felt my eyes burning with hot tears. I stood there holding the kitten and cried for maybe a minute. Then I put the kitten down, wiped my face, and got on with the feeding.

I tipped the right amount of food into the right bowls (some goats get soaked beet shreds, others prefer dry – all very complicated), distributed them, and let Glenda onto the milking stand. She jumped up neatly as always, tucking her nose into the food bowl as I leaned my cheek against her warm, silky flank. I could hear her stomach rumbling as I milked her, the warm liquid squirting and foaming into the jug beneath my hands.

I began to feel, in some small part of my mind, comforted. I gave the goats fresh straw and water, then swept out the barn before heading back indoors. There were things to be done on the computer – urgent deadlines to be met – but first I found myself, almost automatically, measuring out milk to make cheese.

The milk had been stacking up since I'd gone away, and the oldest bottles were starting to go off. I strained the kefir grains out of the goat's milk kefir, used the kefir to blend up a smoothie, which I stashed in the fridge for an after-school snack, added fresh milk to the kefir grains and put it back on the windowsill to ferment.

It was strange – for the first time in days these things didn't seem like a massive effort, or something unfamiliar, but like something that I just did, automatically. It was easier to do it, than *not* to do it. I put the thermometer in the cheese pan and added the cheese starter.

And somewhere, in the washing of milk bottles and the adding of rennet, the straining of the goat's milk kefir and the stirring of the cheese starter, life started to flow back into the tendrils and roots of the vine of my life. I couldn't tell you exactly what, but something shifted. The acid depression started to let go its grip, just a little, and things started – just *started* – to seem possible again.

9 November 2010

An iron-grey day with silver edges, just past Bonfire Night. This is a strange celebration – and so very British – to commemorate a crime that never actually happened! Apparently, back in 1605, a group of men intent on restoring Protestant England to Catholicism plotted to blow up the English Parliament and kill King James I.

One of the conspirators, Guy Fawkes, was captured in the cellars of the House of Lords with several dozen barrels of gunpowder, just before they exploded. All of the conspirators were imprisoned, tortured and killed.

And every year since then, in celebration of the prevention of treason, a 'Guy' is burned in effigy on a huge bonfire lit in every city, town and village. There are fireworks, and children chant this poem:

'Remember, remember, the fifth of November;
Gunpowder, treason and plot;
I see no reason why gunpowder, treason;
Should ever be forgot.'

And they don't forget! Long memories, these British...

I have new company in the kitchen this morning – a beautiful young African grey parrot that we've named Fergie, after the little grey Fergie tractor that's so revered in this country. He looks like a small falcon – hooked beak, dark grey eyes, silvery plumage and a vivid red tail. He has a bright and acute intelligence – different than a human intelligence, but no less sharp. I'm interested in what it'll be like, to share space with a new life form.

I'd asked Rich if he'd mind if we got a parrot, and he agreed, if dubiously. We went to look at one adult parrot listed for sale, and ended up pelting out of the house and along the pavement, while the bird shrieked obscenities as it followed us. So I thought it'd be better if we got a baby parrot. That way, we can teach him what we want him to know. And if he turns out to say swear words, at least they'll be ones that we taught him.

How to Make Cheese

Cheese is just an ancient method
of preserving milk — by getting
rid of all the extra water, and keeping
the proteins that are left behind. Here's the basic
concept of cheese making:

You acidify milk. You can do this with nearly anything —
yogurt, goat's milk kefir, lemon juice, vinegar, cheese starter
(depending on the kind of cheese you want — cheddar
starter, Stilton starter, brie starter, etc.).

You add rennet, to solidify whatever you've got. This results
in a big load of semi-solid stuff that looks like blancmange —
which is called curds — with a watery layer of 'whey' on top.

You spoon the curds into moulds that have holes in them,
leaving as much of the whey behind as possible. The remaining
whey continues to run out of the holes for 24–48 hours,
leaving the increasingly dry 'curd' behind. And that's all
there is to it, really!

How to make cheese with goat's milk kefir

1. Sit goat's milk out in a bowl for 12 hours at room
    temperature, to 'ripen'.

2. Add 30ml (2 tbsp) of goat's milk kefir for each litre
    (1¾ pints) of milk and stir. Wait one hour.

3. Add one drop of rennet per litre (1¾ pints) of milk to 60ml (4tbsp) of pre-boiled, cold water. Add this mixture to the bowl of milk. Stir well.

4. Cover and sit for 12 hours at room temperature. (It doesn't have to be exactly 12 hours — just leave it overnight.)

5. You should now have a 'set'. This is a thin whey on the top and a jelly-like curd substance filling most of the bowl. If you don't have a set, it might be because the room is too cold. Just leave it for longer, until you do have a set.

6. Pour off as much of the whey as possible.

7. Ladle the curd into cheese moulds with holes in them, to allow the whey to drain out. Salt each layer as you go. If you like, you can add mustard seeds, parsley, pepper, chili flakes, dried apricots — whatever you fancy! You can experiment, but stick to dried herbs to start with — fresh ones go brown in the cheese and end up looking horrible! Be creative — Joli once came up with a honey-vanilla goat's cheese that was out of this world.

8. Sit the moulds on a cake cooling rack, over a pan, to drain. (The pan is to catch the whey coming off — the rack to prevent the moulds from sitting in the whey.) Turn the cheese every four hours or so. (Tip it out of the moulds, catch, slide it back in other-way-up. This is a bit messy.)

9. When the curd is dry enough for your taste, move it to the fridge. Enjoy!

The children are enchanted with Fergie; Rich is uncomplaining. I like the sense of company in the kitchen as he sits on his perch, destroying a cluster of seeds with one claw and gazing at me with wise, unfathomable eyes.

Just below Fergie's perch are a box of pineapples and a box of lemons. I bought them from the farmer's market on Friday and am planning an ambitious sort of pineapple-lemon marmalade.

But today on the farm the marmalade is going to have to compete with my soap making. Here's how that started...

A few months ago, we had a surplus of goat's milk backing up in the fridge. Turning to my computer, as I always do, I typed: 'What can I do with goat's milk?' Got all the familiar answers – mostly goat's cheese. Boring – everyone makes it. Moreover, everyone seems to make it better than I do!

But then I saw an entry for goat's milk *soap*. Now that *was* intriguing. Looking a little further, I saw that it was supposed to be good for eczema. Benji had eczema – bingo!

I discovered that it's not completely straightforward, getting the goat's milk into the soap, but it can be done, through a careful freezing process. Where could I learn to make such a thing, I thought? After more searching online, and finding out that making homemade soap involves dealing with hot oil and lye (caustic soda), which can burn or blind you, I figured it might be better to get some expert training before I damaged myself.

I found a marvellous place called Soap School, where a lady named Sarah Janes, and her husband Shawn Dritz, train interested people like myself to make all kinds of delicious homemade soaps, bath bombs, skin creams and the like.

I took a train to London and spent a weekend on a training course with the Soap School, learning to make soap. I enjoyed it so much that then I took another course in Yorkshire, where I learned to put the goat's milk into skin cream. I came home and whipped up a batch of my new concoctions that very afternoon.

I began to use the soap and cream on Benji's skin, and watched carefully over the next few weeks. About three weeks after I began, I looked down at Benji's skin and had to double-check which arm I was looking at – the angry red patch that had been there before was gone.

Was it the same arm? It was. Somehow, unbelievably, the combination of the goat's milk soap and the skin cream combined had cleared Benji's eczema.

I found it hard to credit, but staring down at his perfectly clear skin, I had no choice but to believe it. Cleopatra clearly had been onto something, when she bathed in it – goat's milk was the secret!

Abruptly carried away on a wave on enthusiasm, I started making different flavours of soaps and creams. There was a nearly infinite variety of essential oils that I could add into the basic recipe, each of which has its own individual scent and health benefits, so I was spoiled for choice. Where to begin?

Rosemary essential oil, for example, helps with wrinkles and age spots – and it's also great for itchy, flaky skin. So, I tried making a set of soap and skin cream with rosemary in it. What a lovely scent! Fantastic. I added some organic pink facial clay, and I came up with a pale pink cleansing bar that made my shower smell like a spa.

Let's see, I thought, what else could I make? I was running amok at this point, whizzing round the farmhouse kitchen like a demented bee, stirring up ingredients in my huge stainless-steel jam-making pan, mixing my oils and lotions and potions. Rich would come into the kitchen, raise his eyebrows and back slowly out again.

I thought of the people I love. What would they like? My mum is allergic to everything, even lavender. So, for her, I whipped up a cleansing bar and skin cream with just milk, honey and oatmeal. Completely fragrance-free and non-allergic, I guessed it would be great for kids as well. And for pregnant women, too, since I'd read that they're not supposed to have any essential oils at all.

And our girls? Like most teenagers, they get occasional skin break-outs. What could I make for them? In my reading I came across a scientific study showing that thyme essential oil kills acne bacteria better than benzoyl peroxide, without any of the redness and drying that the nasty chemicals create. Got straight onto Amazon and ordered myself some thyme essential oil!

I added a swig of tea tree essential oil, just for general antibacterial purposes, and came up with a break-out cleanser/skin cream set that works a treat for acne. Something about the combination of the goat's milk, thyme and tea tree essential oils does something magic.

When the girls used it, it took the redness out of their spots in two hours, and cleared their skin in a week. 'Make some more, please!' they begged me, when the first trial pots ran out. So I did.

Pineapple Marmalade

3 sweet oranges

1 lemon

1 large can pineapple chunks (or a fresh pineapple, if you can get it).

1.8kg (4lb) sugar

1. Cut the oranges and lemon (leave the peel on) into very thin slices. Put them in a pan, and just cover with water.

2. Bring to the boil and then simmer until tender.

3. Add the juice from the can of pineapple chunks (or the fresh pineapple) and the finely chopped fruit, and simmer until all the fruit is well blended.

4. Add the sugar, stir until dissolved and then boil rapidly to setting point.

This marmalade is a particular favourite with children, who don't always care for the traditional bitter orange version, and is very good served with steamed puddings or vanilla ice cream.

Some marmalade recipes I've seen recommend that you take out the lemon pips, put them in a muslin bag and boil them along with the fruit. This is to get the pectin into the mix, which is the stuff that makes the jam set properly. It's easy to pull the muslin bag out before you add the sugar.

And then of course there are the gorgeous scents of lavender, lemongrass and spearmint essential oils. Impossible to resist. I love the single strong scents, only one for each kind of soap – I think your body can smell that it's good for you. All those essential oils bring their own healing remedies to the skin, as well as smelling delicious. Why would you ever use artificial perfumes, when essential oils are so amazing?!

So I made soap with those flavours, colouring them soft purples and yellows and greens with alkanet root, calendula and green facial clay. The bars are nice and hard, they don't go stringy and mushy like some hand-made soaps I've tried. And they raise a gorgeous lather.

And the cream is silky and smells lovely as well, sinking into the skin quickly and leaving it feeling soft and healed.

It occurs to me that skin is not so different from the farm. Far from being sterile, the reality is that human skin is covered with trillions of teeming bacteria. And all those life forms need nourishing, just like our animals on the farm. Perhaps the natural ingredients in the skin cream – the milk and natural oils and so on – are actually *feeding* the skin, giving it the nutrients it needs to heal, and that's why the cream works so well on eczema and spots.

Anyhow, I'm really pleased with how it's all turned out! Now I've got batches and batches of soap ready for Christmas, sitting cut up into chunky little bars, all over the kitchen table, wafting their gorgeous scents through the room.

People love them for gifts. But could I really sell them, and make a business out of it? I don't know – I've never been someone who wants to run her own business. A paycheck girl, that's me. I like to do what I do, and let someone else handle the headache of accounting and all that malarkey. I wouldn't have the foggiest idea how to begin to run a business!

But still, there's something tempting about trying....

I'm probably as mad as a box of frogs. Rich would say that I'm *definitely* as mad as a box of frogs.

But, indulgent as ever, he's made me some gorgeous little shelves from reclaimed pine; they look like bird houses. Yesterday we spent a peaceable afternoon together in Rich's wood workshop, as he sawed the shelves to the right length and nailed them together, and I coated the wood with beeswax. The soap will be displayed on the shelves, with a sign that says, 'Homemade soap from the Soap Shak'. (The name's taken from a sign that Joli made for me – that's the original spelling!)

And then I'm going to have to summon up the courage to walk into shops in this area and ask them if they'll sell it... not a prospect that I'm looking forward to.

Today, I have to wrestle with the labelling for the soap packaging. EU regulations dictate that it all has to be done just so – Latin names of ingredients included. It's intimidating.

So, after the milking of the goats and the feeding of the pigs and the sheep that are being fattened in the top shed, it's back into the kitchen to chop up those pineapples and lemons, put the marmalade on to boil, and straight into writing the soap labels.

23 November 2010

It's been a time of high romance on the farm! All the nanny goats are coming into season, and we, like all the other goat owners in the area, have been scrambling around trying to solve the billy problem.

The billy problem is this – male goats are big, and they smell atrocious. (For the record, female goats kept in tidy conditions smell lovely, a bit like cinnamon.) And most people don't want to keep male goats around.

Since you only really need the males once a year, to put the does in kid so that you can milk them, it makes more sense to have just a few billies around. Then you can transport the females to the males when it's time, as I did back in September.

In practice, there are fewer and fewer goat keepers in our area. Goat-keeping seems to have had its heyday back in the late 70s, with *The Good Life,* a popular British TV show, and it's been dwindling ever since. So there are fewer males around than there used to be, and each year this problem dawns with a new intensity on the owners of nannies – who absolutely *have* to find a billy!

You'd think that there'd be an organized registry of male goats standing at stud, and of course there is. The British Goat Society keeps one, and so does the Anglo-Nubian Breed Society. But those males tend to be a six-, eight- or even 10-hour drive away – and although we love our goats, we don't love them quite that much.

So we fall back on the old word-of-mouth system, wherein you ring someone and ask them if they know of anyone who has a billy. The Welsh jungle drums… and they're remarkably effective.

This year we ended up borrowing a billy from a friend to take our Anglo-Nubian girls on – ahem – 'dates'. Poor Hercules the billy. He was very young – if well-intentioned – and if he were human, he would have glasses, spots and buckteeth. He manfully did his best, but our glossy girls were about twice his size, and they would look at him, look at me and then roll their eyes, as if to say, 'Is this as good as it gets?'

But the thing about Hercules is that he was so easy to handle, and so easily intimidated himself, that I found myself changing my mind about males. They're not so bad. They're not so scary. And the weirdest thing of all – I kind of like the way they smell. Strange, I know. Suddenly, keeping our own male was sounding better and better.

And then Rich kept looking at these two Saanen males for sale on a website. He just liked the look of them, he said. And then he announced his intention to expand the Saanen part of the herd because, as he says, 'If Glenda had fingers, she would milk herself.' Glenda, our Saanen, is without a doubt the most reliable, placid creature in existence. (If – don't listen Glenda – a bit dull. I prefer the splash and verve of the Anglo-Nubians. If Saanens are like carthorses, Nubies are like thoroughbreds.)

Anyhow, all of this added up to the fact that last Friday, we found ourselves in the car, trailer hitched behind, driving three hours up into North Wales to go and pick up this Saanen billy. He's a handsome thing, with a majestic beard and a winning smile. Rich dubbed him Snowdon, both for his white coat and the famous mountain in North Wales by the same name.

Snowdon was duly installed in the goat barn, and now, we figure, we just need one more male to make our lives complete. An Anglo-Nubian this time. We've heard there's one for sale in Cambridge, just a five-hour drive away. Hmmm... Goats seem to be a growing addiction with us. And an expensive one, at that. I wonder, could they ever *make* us money, instead of *costing* us money all the time?

26 November 2010

Fat white flakes falling this morning, sky grey as smoke, and the snow lying thick on the yard, going crick underfoot with that satisfying crunch that tells you it'd pack into a perfect snowball. A white goose in the goose run beats his wings in the white snow, suddenly, like a very small archangel.

The barn is warm this morning, filled with hay and the breath of animals, all bleating and mooing and wanting their breakfast. We've heard from the National Trust farm in Cambridge, and they're going to sell us their Anglo-Nubian billy. Hooray. Rich will set out on the day-long drive to pick it up on Monday (weather permitting!), while I stay home and grapple with children, animals and farm chores. I wish I could go with Rich, but someone needs to stay behind and feed all the waiting mouths.

I've just read something so lovely that I want to write it down whole, so that I can try and understand it. It was written by

Sister Miriam Therese MacGillis, a Dominican nun who lives in a place called Genesis Farm in the USA, where they practise something called 'sacred agriculture'.

Sister MacGillis starts with a quote from the Irish scholar and priest Vincent McNabb: 'If there's one truth more than any other, which life and thought have made us admit, against our prejudices, and even against our will, it's that there's little hope of saving civilization or religion except by the return of contemplatives to the land.'

She goes on to say that if we understand the Earth as a living being that exists to regenerate and transform itself, then the role of farmer would be raised to a sacred profession... that farmers act in a prophetic role, entering the sanctuary of the soil and engaging with the forces of creation. She says that the soils, microbes and animals are all revelatory and holy... and that if we understood it all this way, our obsessions with control and power would disappear.

And she ends with this ringing call: 'Let the contemplatives return to the land.' I love it!

6 December 2010

A landscape of silver, copper and diamonds this morning, like the fairy tale of the Dancing Princesses. The beeches in the hedge have hung on to their leaves, rust and ochre-coloured, and a thick layer of frost has bleached and rimed all the twigs and grass and low-slung hills, like a coating of glass reflecting back a pale, bright blue sky.

It all looks very lovely, but on the farm, the reality of a hard frost is that the outside spring tap has frozen solid and water has to be carried from the house, one bucket at a time, out to the animals. Each pen of pigs, goats and sheep needs the dirty water bucket to be thawed and emptied – to be replaced with clean, warm water. And since we're now up to 10 goats that means quite a few trips.

We have a lovely new male goat, a billy called Wilburforce. He's dark chocolate brown with a black stripe down his shoulders and back – very handsome and dignified. He's settled straight into his new pen, munching his hay happily and looking around with glazed pleasure at all the nanny goats, whom he confidently expects to be romancing before too long.

We haven't broken it to him yet, but since they're all already in kid, he won't be getting any action until around this time next year. Still, from the look in his eye, you can tell that he's dreaming winter dreams.

The inside of the barn is now absolutely packed, and swelling with expectant life – we're hoping that all seven of the nannies are in kid. We could have as many as 21 goat kids come the spring! Marmite the Toggie princess is due to pop first, in February. She's getting big and slow, and I find her lying down in the morning when I come in to feed – very unlike her usual pushy self.

It's easier to understand what the poets always say about the growth of spring hiding inside the death of winter, when I think of the barn filled with pregnant goats, warm with living creatures and fresh straw, and shuttered against the cold frost outside.

I came home from my business trip to Copenhagen last Friday (four airports, three airplanes, three hours in the car), just as our good friends Chris and Justine arrived at the farm with their three children. Justine works with Rich at the Harp Centre, and she and Chris are a lovely couple. Our oldest girl, Ceris, had agreed to babysit the kids while we adults all went out to the harp's Christmas party.

The noise and preparations as we all got dressed were nearly as much fun as the party. And I must say that we all became fabulously glamorous in no time flat! Then Ceris's boyfriend, George, acted as our taxi and ferried us to the party; he came and got us later, too, when we were all slightly the worse for wear. Bless him.

We woke up with some difficulty the next morning. Then Joli, Ceris, Justine and I formed a little cottage industry production line at the kitchen table, wrapping and packaging 44 bars of my homemade goat's milk soap, as we laughed and talked over the evening before. Each bar gets tied with raffia, affixed with a label explaining that it's all natural, and has a star anise hot-glued to the bow.

Looks lovely, but it's a bit fiddly, so it was wonderful to have all the extra hands. The smell of mint, lemongrass and lavender wafted through the room, and the Alpha range, purring and grumbling, made the kitchen blissfully warm.

Then it was off to the Christmas fair at Pontgarreg, where we set the soap up on a table and waited with bated breath to see if anyone would buy it. Two stores in the area are stocking my soap, but this was the first time I really had a chance to see people handling and smelling and deciding whether to buy, and

I was eager to see the results. Joli and Ceris came with me, to take turns minding the stall.

For the first 45 minutes, we sat miserably quiet, and didn't sell a single bar, while people all around us were selling things like crazy. It was horrible – like being a wallflower at a dance, when everyone else is being asked. I was about to give up and go home, to spare myself further humiliation, but then someone bought one bar, and then another, and by the end of the day we'd sold 31 bars – nearly three-quarters of our stock!

It was flying off the table. People seemed to love the soap; they put in requests for new flavours, and asked where they could buy more. I was terribly pleased and relieved, and full of plans to move ahead. Could this ever become a business, I wondered again? Something that we could do from the farm – a way that the goats could help us make a living?

8 December 2010

The frost has lost its novelty, but the bone-hard freeze lingers on... and on. The barn chores take twice the time they normally do, because of the pails of water that have to be hauled from the house out to each stall – a shoulder-wrenching job.

Today I thought with envy of the antique wooden yokes I've seen in museums – they fit over your shoulders, so that you can dangle a bucket from each end without having to bear the weight on your arms. I finally really understand what they're for. And I want one to make the chores easier. Maybe Rich could make me one.

The sheep in the top field need bales of hay taken out to them (a wheelbarrow job for me – Rich can just sling one up on his shoulder) and the goats are looking wistful in their stalls, missing their galloping, leaping romps down the long goat hill into the woods. But it's too cold for them, and they wouldn't be able to eat enough of the frozen grass stubble to make up the calories they would burn off. No, better that they stay inside in the warm barn and eat the hay from the summer. And incubate the goat kids they're carrying.

Taking each bale of hay from the neat stack in the hay barn, and parcelling it out into the hay racks, gives me the same feeling as when I open a jar of homemade blackberry jam, bottled in the summer and opened in the depths of winter.

When the first waft of sweet fragrance escapes from the jar, it's as if all the days of late summer – the slanting golden light, the harvest and fresh tomatoes, the days on the beach, Rich, bare-chested, swinging his tractor in wide arcs across the field, the fêtes and fairs, and stallions galloping down the high street of Cardigan – come rushing back, preserved in the jam like amber.

And the hay is the same. We watched it grow through the spring – fed it with the muck of last year's lambs – checked it carefully every day, as the purple heads of the wild herbs came to just the right point of goodness. Waited anxiously for the rain to stop and the rare patch of three days' worth of sun to coincide with the ripeness of the hay.

Rich cut the hay on the tractor and baled it, and we all laboured, with the hot sun beating down on our backs, slinging the bales up onto the tractor. And all those memories, that time and effort, the stamp of this place, is in every bale that I pull down and cut open and distribute to the goats.

The goats eat the hay, and their muck will go back out onto the fields to grow next year's hay. A commonplace phenomenon, and one that's taken entirely for granted in this part of the world. But I never get tired of feeling around the edges of this experience, and marvelling at it.

You know, it's strange, but I was just thinking today – as I tried futilely to tidy the barn without any running water – I've been on the radio speaking to more than a million listeners and I've written award-winning stories for a newspaper; I've written a novel and appeared on television; I've been photographed for a poster, and picked up in a limousine to give a speech, but I always felt that I wasn't doing *quite what I was meant to do.*

I tried to fix it. I looked for causes to support and ways to make a difference in the world, thinking that might help. I tried different topics and formats and ideas on my radio show, thinking that I just hadn't yet found my voice. I kept waiting to climb just that one little notch higher on the career ladder, so that I'd finally slot into place – into my place, the one that was meant for me. If I was doing what I was designed to do, I reckoned, that nagging sense of being – well, slightly out of place – would go away.

There's a portrait of me, painted by Danni Dawson – a brilliantly talented artist friend of my parents – when I was 12 years old. It has a particularly penetrating, level gaze. When the picture hung over my fireplace in California, I often had the impulse to turn it towards the wall, to escape it. 'What have you done with my life?' the painted face would seem to ask, accusingly. And I didn't have an answer – not really.

But here, for the first time, as I struggled to chip dirty, frozen straw out of the wheelbarrow with a shovel, to make room for another load of dirty straw, I realized that I don't feel like I'm wasting my time any more. I don't feel like I'm spinning my wheels.

I'm finally, in fact, doing what I was always meant to do. I could face that portrait of my 12-year-old self now, and she'd understand.

She would approve. She might even smile.

Funny, isn't it? It's all about *change*.

I've come to believe that the whole lot – life, the universe and everything – is just a bunch of energy changing from form to form. At the moment, this energy is pig-formed – when it turns into food, and I take in the food, the energy will be me-formed. And in the end, that form, too, will vanish. Dancing from one form to another.

As farmers, we have our hands on those changes. We're present at the cusp of one thing turning into another. Life, into death, at this very moment. And we're present at the beginning of life – the breeding of the goats, the birthing of the lambs, the planting of the seeds. The magic is in the transitions. We're those lucky ones who are privileged to preside over the change points – where one thing becomes another.

It's the same with making our own food – there are all these magical transformations. The point where goat's milk magically solidifies into curds, for cheese. The point where the living yeast makes the flour turn into bread. The point where the bones and water and vegetables magically become cawl. The point where the seed becomes the tomato plant.

It's about transformation – the pigs go from living to dead, and then into sausages. Magic is all about dramatic points of change. Benji said so in the car this morning, when we were talking about getting milk from the goats:

'That's magic, isn't it?'

'That's right,' I told him. 'What else is magic?'

'When a sheep has a baby lamb.'

'Right! What else?'

'When a baby seed grows into a plant.'

'Good boy! And what else?'

'When Daddy makes a shed out of nothing.'

Benji has got it nailed – and he's only five years old.

There's no *change* in the plastic-wrapped food that I buy from the shop. It sits in eternal twilight, mummified, until it finally, gingerly, goes a little mushy and I throw it away.

Like living wrapped in plastic, in a plastic house, working in a plastic cubicle. I remember living like that. Nothing much ever changed. People in that world seem to want to remain the same, as well. To stay forever young – lurking in a state of stale semi-hibernation.

But for me, it's putting my hands on the points of transformation that makes things exciting. That's where you find the juice, the passionate engagement, the dance.

My boss, who works in a strictly corporate environment and prefers to hire out even the mowing of his own lawn grass, was curious about how we handle all the work on the farm.

'Doesn't Rich work full-time?' he asked. 'Do you take care of all the animals and the kids by yourself?'

'No, we do it together,' I told him. 'We both work; we both take care of the kids; we both take care of the animals.'

'Aren't you just scrambling all the time?'

'We're not scrambling,' I said. 'We're dancing.'

14 February 2011

A day of firsts. The first snowdrop, white and fragile against the soaked brown bracken. And our first goat kid – Valentine – born silvery grey and white, perfectly patterned, with Nancy Sinatra-style white boots and elegant stripes down each side of her head. The first goat kid born into the Hoffnant herd. Her mother, Marmite, looked ridiculously pleased and licked her all over. We hung over the stable door, marvelling and admiring. What a clever girl Marmite is.

My friend Sue phoned me in great excitement today. 'Turn on the Food Show, on BBC Radio 4!' she cried. 'There's a doctor on there talking about raw milk, like your goat's milk!' I flipped on the radio straight away. The doctor being interviewed was Dr Natasha Campbell-McBride, a noted neurologist and one of the world's leading experts in treating children and adults with learning disabilities and mental, digestive and immune disorders. I was so interested in what she was saying that I wrote it down:

'Milk as it leaves the animal is alive, because it is, in effect, the white blood of the animal with red blood cells removed. It contains active, alive lymphocytes, macrophages, neutrophils, antibodies, and other immune cells which kill infection, and protect us from infection. It has active, alive enzymes and vitamins, in the best biochemical shape and form for the human body to assimilate.

'Raw milk is a probiotic food, with lactobacilli, bifidobacteria and other probiotic bacteria. All these substances are there for a purpose – to protect the milk from contamination and infection – so raw, alive milk, as it leaves the animal, is protected from infection.

'All that protection is conferred to the person, when they drink it in that shape and form. When we pasteurize milk, we kill it. The immune cells are killed; the enzymes are destroyed; the probiotic bacteria are killed. This becomes a dead, processed product, coming into your digestive system. It's very hard work for your digestive system and body to handle. Alive, raw milk is equipped with all the factors for us to digest lactose in the best possible way, so it does our digestive tract only good.

'When we pasteurize milk, we destroy all those factors. So lactose becomes hard to digest, and people become lactose intolerant. They develop bloating, diarrhoea, abdominal cramps, and other unpleasant symptoms. I find that many lactose intolerant patients, when they start drinking raw milk, can tolerate it perfectly well.'

Wow! We knew that the raw goat's milk was good stuff, and we knew that it'd cured Benji's bronchial infections, but until now, we didn't know exactly what we had, or why it was working – or that it's so important the milk is raw.

I sat down and ordered a copy of Dr Campbell-McBride's book, *Gut and Psychology Syndrome: Natural Treatment for Autism, ADHD/ADD, Dyslexia, Dyspraxia, Depression, and Schizophrenia*. My journalist's 'news nose' told me that there was something here worth following up.

27 February 2011

Sing a song of small things... It occurs to me suddenly that the problem is not the galaxy out there, it's the galaxy in *here*.

I'm carrying Dr Campbell-McBride's book everywhere with me, reading it word for word, turning the pages in fascination, despite the fact that I don't have a scientific bone in my body. She's so clear about what's going on inside the body. I've never read such a simple, easy explanation of physical science. I was particularly struck by the following passage:

Shann's Magic Cawl

Experience the slow magic of watching leftover bones turn into delicious stew. Cawl is simply a traditional Welsh meat stew and it's easy to make. You start with any meat that has the bone still in. It's a great thing to make on a Monday after a Sunday roast — it will absorb all your leftovers. The secret to a good cawl is time — it can happily simmer away on its own, without any input from you — the key is simply to start it going early enough in the day. This recipe serves 4–6.

Leftover roast meat with bones (a chicken carcass, beef, or lamb by choice — I find that pork doesn't work so well, as it's too greasy). The bone should be cracked so that the marrow can escape into the broth.

2 tsp salt	3 onions	1 swede
5 whole black peppercorns	4 carrots	1 leek
	4 potatoes	

1. Put the meat into a big pan, fill three-quarters full of water, and then add the salt and the peppercorns. Bring to the boil and then lower the heat to a simmer.

2. Simmer for at least two hours, although the longer

the better! Check periodically to make sure the pan hasn't boiled dry, and add more water if needed.

3. Put a colander into another large pan, and sieve the broth into the new pan, leaving the bones and meat in the colander. Put the broth back on the stove top and return to a simmer. Allow the meat and bones to cool.

4. Peel and roughly chop the onions, carrots, potatoes and swede. Pop them into the broth. Simmer for another two hours.

5. Once the meat has cooled enough to handle, pull the slivers of meat off the bones, chop and add to the broth. Discard the bones.

6. Thirty minutes before the cawl is served, slice the leek and add it to the pot. Turn off the heat 10 minutes before suppertime and allow the cawl to cool slightly.

Traditionally, cawl was eaten in wooden bowls, with wooden spoons. It was served in two courses — the broth and veg first, and the meat after. As a real peasants' dish, the idea was to fill everyone up on the veg first, and serve the meat more sparingly! But we just eat ours all together. It's the ultimate leftovers soup — and it's even better on the 'second boil', when you reheat it the following day.

Rich likes to put slices of sharp cheddar cheese in his cawl bowl, and let it go all melty in the soup. Yumm...

'A human body is like a planet inhabited by huge numbers of various micro-creatures. The diversity and richness of this life on every one of us is probably as amazing as the life on Earth itself. Our digestive system, skin, eyes, respiratory and excretory organs are happily co-existing with trillions of invisible lodgers, making one ecosystem of macro- and micro-life, living together in harmony. It's a symbiotic relationship, where neither party can live without the other.

'Let me repeat this: we humans cannot live without these tiny microorganisms, which we carry on and in our bodies everywhere. The largest colonies of microbes live in our digestive system. A healthy adult on average carries 1.5–2 kg (3–4lb) of bacteria in the gut. All these bacteria are not just a chaotic microbial mass, but a highly organized micro-world with certain species predominating and controlling others. The number of functions they fulfil in our bodies are so vital to us, that if our gut got sterilized, we would probably not survive.'

So, we are a planet, hosting innumerable life forms. Our ancestors co-existed happily with tiny, invisible microorganisms. They made use of them to create food, in the form of sourdough starter, yeast and cheese culture.

Cheese is made with rennet, which is the lining of a calf's stomach. You take the rennet and put it into milk, to start the curds forming. The reason this works is that the microorganisms from the calf's gut help it digest its mother's milk. You take those bugs and put them in the milk; you are essentially borrowing the calf's ability to digest the milk. The calf is extending its protection to you.

In the past, humans lived happily with the world of microorganisms. Then we got smart enough to see these bugs in a microscope, and we were horrified. We called them germs, and set out to kill as many as possible. We tried to sanitize everything – surfaces, food products, soil, milk, the lot. Blast the bugs and the weeds with pesticides, and then put chemicals back in to make the plants grow. Processed food loses its taste, flavour and colour, so chemical additives are added to compensate.

We know now what the result of that has been. Sanitize a child's environment too energetically, and you'll create allergies. Feed generations of children processed food and you have an epidemic of autism, ADHD, eczema and asthma.

The next step for human beings, I think, is this one – learn to understand the world of microorganisms, and co-exist with it.

Dr Campbell-McBride went on to crystallize her findings into something called the GAPS diet (Gut and Psychology Syndrome), which has helped hundreds of thousands of people all over the world suffering from autism, dyspraxia, ADD, dyslexia, ADHD, schizophrenia and depression.

Turns out that all these patients have something in common: they struggle with digestive problems – abnormal flora in the gut. This creates 'leaky' gut walls that don't process food properly. So the patients are not only suffering from malnutrition, but food molecules that aren't converted properly escape into the blood system, where they affect the brain, causing abnormal behaviour.

The GAPS diet basically works on a two-part principle: first heal the lining of the gut, then repopulate it with good flora. You heal the gut by eating homemade meat stocks (boiling meat bones in water releases cartilaginous material that helps the healing process). You then repopulate the good flora with homemade yogurt and kefir.

Here's an extraordinary thing. Rich suffers from ulcerative colitis, and we'd just got to the point where we went to see a specialist in London. He told us that there was no more help for it; Rich would have to have a colostomy. We were horrified.

But when we returned home, Rich went into spontaneous – and complete – remission. He's been entirely symptom free ever since. We were so relieved by the timely miracle that we didn't think that much about it. It was simply, grace.

But now I realize that the GAPS diet is exactly what I've been feeding Rich for the last three years. We butcher our own meat and put it in the freezer. To cook it, I hoist it into a pan of water and cook it all day on the Alpha, because it's too big to thaw in the microwave. So he's been getting a lot of homemade meat stocks.

And, as we had so much goat's milk, I started making yogurt and goat's milk kefir, just as a way to use up the excess milk. So he was getting the good flora, as well.

We'd accidentally stumbled on the diet designed to help him – just from eating the way that people always have, on the farm! These are the ways that people used to eat, when tiny microorganisms were a part of everyday life. I've a jar of sourdough starter in the fridge. The living organism in it will make my bread rise. I've a container of goat's milk kefir fermenting on the table. The life in it will repopulate our guts with good flora, and keep us healthy.

Like learning to co-exist with the world outside, we have to learn to co-exist with the world inside – all the trillions of tiny living cells living on us and in us without which we could not exist. We are the planet. Literally.

Fired by this discovery, Rich and I began to seriously discuss the possibility of trying to start our own business. Maybe there was a market for the goat's milk goodies that have been so healing for our own family. If raw goat's milk is such a powerful health product, perhaps we could become licensed to sell it?

If goat's milk kefir is so helpful to children with autism, maybe there are parents out there who'd like to buy it – to have it made for them, rather than having to make it themselves?

Maybe we could make it here on the farm, for other families, the way we've been making it for our own family?

16 March 2011

Okay. We're going to try it. We're probably crazy. In fact, we're *definitely* crazy! But we're going to give it a go. Since we have the goats and love them and milk them anyway – as a very expensive hobby – it makes a certain kind of nutty sense that if we push it a little further, it might actually give us something back. It might, in fact, earn us a living. A brave and dangerous thought, in a time when farming seems doomed to fail, and everyone accepts that smallholdings don't make money.

But we've decided to try.

So now we're struggling to get a new barn built and a brand-new, start-from-scratch dairy up and running. I signed up for a free 'start-your-own-business' class, where I spent three days trying to wrap my mind around the complexities of tax exemptions, business costings and marketing plans. We've registered with Farming Connect, who are going to provide us with some discounted training and a 'Whole Farm' mentor.

Rich has been working every hour in the day, trying to expand the barn and create a milking parlour that will keep the hygiene inspector happy. And my cousin Ron has flown over from Texas to help with the backbreaking work of barn-building. He's lovely – it feels like he's always been with us.

22 March 2011

Everything is a disaster at the moment! The first ewe has had lambs, but she doesn't seem interested in feeding them. So we've got two baby lambs in the kitchen that need feeding four times a day.

Marmite, who's the only goat milking at the moment (16 goats and only one in milk – some dairy!) has developed mastitis, and has an oozing sore on her udder. Rich wheeled her off to the vets in the trailer as soon as he came home, and the vet says she'll have to be pumped full of all kinds of antibiotics, which means we can't use her milk – which leaves us without milk of any kind. So I'll have to buy it from the shop – which I hate doing!

I have to travel to Denmark tomorrow for four days – I don't want to go, but we desperately need the cash infusion to pay for the renovation of the barn and to set up the dairy. I've made lists and more lists of things for everyone to do in my absence – but Rich is looking boot-faced, and with all the animals poorly and needing feeding, it's going to be a nightmare for him.

Yesterday Rich and I were in the kitchen until 11 p.m., and looked at each other in despair – is it always going to be this hard?

'We knew this was going to be the difficult bit,' I reminded him. 'The overlap – where we're working to get the dairy going, while still doing our other jobs. It won't always be this bad.'

'If it's always this bad,' he replied grimly, 'we're not going to keep doing it.'

26 March 2011

I went to Denmark: training executives to do public speaking in a majestic country mansion decorated with glistening chandeliers and grey velvet furnishings. Came home to find that Joli had made a delicious rabbit pie and homemade biscuits, cleaned the kitchen, swept the porch and put a jug of wild daffodils on the kitchen table. And she's only 12 years old! It's heaven to be home.

The barn is looking gorgeous; white-washed walls for the pens, light and airy, windows to let in the sun, neat milking benches, a milking parlour, a dairy to process the fresh milk. Unbelievable that Rich has managed to put all this together on a shoestring, with no deep pockets, no investors, nothing but his own skill and hard work.

He's done all the designing, digging, plumbing, electrics, building, roofing, automatic watering systems. I marvel at him, all over again. He has the brain of a skilled engineer and the hands of a master craftsman. We could never have afforded to hire someone to create the barn and the milking system for us. His abilities have made it possible for us to try to launch this business.

30 March 2011

All hell has broken loose in the barn – the goats are kidding right, left and centre. Teasel had triplets – black ones with white noses and long snowstorm ears. They're tiny and skinny, with long spidery legs. Joli loves them, since Teasel is her goat. We'd just decided that Conkers wasn't pregnant after all, when she popped out a single kid with gorgeous colouring – fawn brown with dark eel stripes. It's strong and stocky and lovely, and undoubtedly the most beautiful kid yet.

Rich constructed a wooden kid pen up at the top of the hay barn, where the kids are warm and cosy, protected from the weather and far enough away from their anxious mothers that they can't hear each other bleat. They have to be separated from their moms, so that we can milk the mothers, and the bond between them is broken. When they stop calling for each other, the kids can all go into one pen together inside the barn.

Another aspect of the whole business that seems heartless – but it's a reality of dairy farming life. You have to produce a baby animal to get the milk to flow – but the baby can't be allowed to drink all the milk if you want to have any to sell. Luckily, if the babies are taken away from the mothers, the mothers produce much more milk than if they were left on, so there's enough to feed the kids and us, too. And, hopefully, some members of the paying public... if our little infant business is ever going to get off the ground.

2 April 2011

More bad news – it feels like we're swimming the English Channel, and just getting smacked in the face with wave after wave of salt water. Rich's Land Rover has packed in, and he thinks it's completely dead. We need it to tow the goat trailer, pull out stuck tractors and all sorts of other tasks. Can't manage without it. Can't afford to replace it. Don't know what we're going to do – we've had two cars die in the time we've been trying to launch this new business – and the money to replace this one will suck up every pound that we've saved to outfit the new dairy! Argh!

My dad has been an angel and come to the rescue. He's giving me my birthday gift early, to bail us out with the car. And, he says, he's throwing in extra to act as start-up for the business. A life raft in the middle of the bitter water! And Rich's dad says that he'll help us out, as well. Feeling so grateful for a loving family... immediate crisis weathered. But frightening long-term implications – we're on such a shoestring, trying to fund this business out of our very shallow pockets, that any little setback can completely derail us.

On the upside, we went into Cardigan today to speak with our business advisor. I've been working like a demon on a business plan and grant application, and he says it looks good, and that he sees no reason why we shouldn't get the EU grant that we've applied for. It's not a lot of money – and we have to put in 60 per cent to their 40 per cent – but it'd be so reassuring to think that the government believes our business idea is viable enough to invest in. Fingers crossed. He's sent off our application, and we should hear one way or another before too long.

5 April 2011

Went into the barn today to try to milk Seren again. She kidded five days ago – twins, a beautiful black nanny with white speckled ears and silver splotches on her body, and a male with the same colouring. He got put down. But Seren, normally so affectionate and even-tempered, isn't taking very well to being milked. She kicks over the bucket, refuses to eat the food in front of her, and generally drives everyone crazy. So I've been ending up covered with milk, shouting, sweating and swearing, just trying to get some milk out so that she won't go rock-hard and get mastitis. It's a mess.

I thought that I'd go out at the half-point in the day, and try to get a little more out of her. Otherwise, by night-time her udder will be tight as a drum with milk, and painful, which won't make the whole process any easier.

I also had to feed the kids. We've got some who get fed five times a day, some who get fed four times a day, and others still who get fed three times a day, so I'm out there a lot. Anyhow, I went out, casually looking to the right and left of the whitewashed stalls as I walked by, automatically checking on all the goats. And when I got to Buddug's stall I did a double take – she had two kids in with her! She's not due for another week, so she hasn't even moved into the 'keeping an eye on her' phase. I went in closer for a look, heart pounding excitedly.

Buddug is the only goat whose billy we'd consider keeping – she's from a different line than everyone else, so he'd be unrelated to the rest of the flock, and thus good breeding material. Plus, our friend Aeron, who shows prize-winning goats and likes black goats especially, had put in a word that he might be interested in a male from her.

Both of Buddug's kids had black bodies with silver splotches, and white speckled ears, in what looked to be the characteristic Hoffnant pattern this season. But my stomach sank as I looked closer at one of them. Something was wrong with his face – terribly wrong. His nose was deformed, more like a trunk. And his tongue lolled out of the side of his mouth. Otherwise, he was big, healthy, beautifully marked, sturdy.

I went in and picked up the other one, examined her. A girl. I sprayed her dangling umbilical cord with iodine, dyeing my hands yellow. The little nanny screamed and struggled in my hands. Something long and wet slapped the back of my arm, and I looked up in shock.

Buddug was eating the afterbirth (as all prey animals do, to avoid leaving a blood trail), which drooped out of her mouth like a slimy, gory piece of pasta. Hearing her kid call, she'd swung her head around and smacked me with the long, dangling thing. I'm surely going to be sick now, I thought. But I wasn't.

Then Buddug dropped the afterbirth, which draped itself neatly over the shoulders of the deformed male kid. He staggered under its weight, and cried out. If my hands hadn't been so goopy, I would have put my head in my hands and cried. But I couldn't – they were covered with slime, iodine and purple foot-spray. Just as well – crying wouldn't have been any use.

I went indoors to wash my hands and get a pair of gloves. I wasn't prepared to handle that afterbirth with my bare hands, even after three years on the farm. But I couldn't leave it wrapped around the little billy. By the time I came back, the afterbirth was gone – mercifully vacuumed up by Buddug.

When Benji came home, he was overjoyed to hear that Buddug had had a girl. He went straight out to see her and came in to announce that her name would be Daisy. A good name. The little male will have to be put down.

6 April 2011

Brutal day today – I was up at 6 a.m., and on the road for a two-hour drive to Cardiff, where I spent all day taking an intensive bookkeeping course on software called QuickBooks, so that I can keep our business accounts. An endeavour as foreign to me as flying to the moon! As my artistic mother says with horror, 'It's not in your DNA!' And she's right. But I find that you can do an awful lot that's not in your DNA, with a bit of determination.

I drove home and arrived to find that Rich had brought in a big load of sand to render out the dairy, fixed his Land Rover (the one we thought was dead!) and got the milk machine going, so that it milked out the nightmarish Seren in two minutes flat.

Ron had been up on the scaffolding, painting the house, bless him. And feeding all the baby animals, of whom there are many at the moment. Another lamb had been born while I was gone. It needed nursing, so we brought it inside by the Alpha, warmed it up, wrapped it in a towel and fed it some of the extra colostrum that we milked off Buddug – since she had twins and the poor little male didn't make it, she's got twice as much as she needs, so we milked off the yellow creamy stuff and stashed it in the freezer. A tiny tub of it goes for £22 in the freeze-dried powder form, so we have riches stored away!

Wednesday is supposed to be our date night, but it was 9.20 p.m. by the time we were finished with all the animals, so Rich and I just called it a day and stumbled to bed. Tomorrow I have another class to get me up to snuff on business skills – this one on taxes.

15 April 2011

Getting licensed to sell raw goat's milk has turned out to be a major challenge! I started out by phoning the council, the Department for Food and Rural Affairs (DEFRA) – anyone I could think of who might have information. The council, in particular, was irritatingly unhelpful.

'I'd like to get licensed to sell raw goat's milk,' I told the woman on the other end of the phone. 'Can you steer me to the appropriate department?'

'I don't know,' she said.

'Riiiiight,' I said. 'Can you let me speak to someone who might know?'

'I don't know,' she said again.

'Can you even tell me which government body handles this sort of thing? Where I should begin to make enquiries?'

'No.'

I hung up and phoned the Grants from the goat club. Ian gave us the name of his dairy inspector. I phoned this person, and he gave me the name of our local inspector. I phoned *that* person, and asked him to come round.

Turns out he was a very nice young bloke named Mike.

'Mike,' I said, refilling his mug with tea. 'Why was it so hard for me to find you?'

'Well,' he said, 'they'd like to ban raw milk altogether. But as they can't, they just make it as difficult as possible.'

Unfortunately for the powers that be, opposition just hardens my resolve. If I wasn't determined before, I certainly was now! I pressed on.

Eventually the facts began to emerge from the confusing red-tape muddle. We needed two different kinds of inspectors: one to inspect the process from animal to tank and another from tank to gate. I found and contacted the second inspector, asking the advice of both as we set up the dairy and milking system. We got a lot of good advice from them, and because we involved the inspectors in the process, we were able to set things up properly from the beginning. I phoned them and phoned them, until they begged me to stop contacting them. Rather too much inspection than too little, I figured!

And finally, we were there. We were done. TB-tested, brucellosis-free, barns inspected, HACCP (Hazard Analysis And Critical Control Points) in place. Milk micro-checked, paperwork in order. Licensed, registered and legal to sell raw goat's milk! I've done a lot of difficult things in my life, but I truly think that whipping the paperwork involved in this project was the most difficult. But very, very satisfying.

We invited some friends around, cracked open a bottle of wine, and after a long and hilarious evening, we came up with a name for the business. Not Laughing Goat – too much like Laughing Cow. Smiling Goat – too milky, Giggling Goat – too silly. But how about chuckling? Babies chuckle, brooks chuckle, wise men chuckle. So be it: Chuckling Goat was born.

25 May 2011

Things have been spinning so fast that I haven't had a chance to write my diary! We've actually sold our first few pints of milk – I was so proud as I looked at them lined up like little soldiers. They got loaded into Taid's old orange cool box and away we went – five to the farm shop in Sarnau, five to the health food shop in Newcastle Emlyn. They seem to be selling pretty well – we now have some more in the Carrot Cruncher store in Newcastle Emlyn, and got word that another shop in Aberporth wants them as well.

It's such tiny money – four and five pounds at a time – but I carefully keep track of it in the envelope where our weekly takings are recorded. Small acorns, small acorns, I chant under my breath. Keep the mighty oak in the mind's eye, and don't get discouraged.

In the meantime, we've finalized the packaging for the soap. It's lovely – unbleached cotton bags with a drawstring and the logo, inspired by an old Celtic symbol, on the front. The bags cost a huge whack of money – so I'm holding my breath that it'll all work, and we'll earn the money back. I want to find some new silicon moulds for the soap that have our symbol on them.

And I need to make some soap to sell! And the labels keep coming back with typos and errors!

In the meantime (the *other* meantime?), I've spent two days at Food Centre Wales at Horeb, with the fantastic team there, trying to develop our probiotic kefir smoothies. We spend two and a half hours slowly and tortuously bringing the goat's milk up to a boil, stirring it the whole time. The result was a nasty mess that tasted like goat sick, and all the flavourings I'd brought with me didn't disguise the horrible goaty flavour.

When I asked Margaret Grant what I'd done wrong, she laughed. 'I always just whack it up on high heat, boil it as fast as possible, then simmer for 15 minutes. Heating it slowly like that just gives the bacteria time to develop, and will make it taste horrible. Stirring it the whole time batters it – just boil it quick and leave it alone!' So much for data sheets. I'll stick with Mrs Grant's advice from now on.

Good news is that I contacted Dr Natasha Campbell-McBride, the wonderful doctor who wrote the book about the GAPS diet that seems to have worked so well for Rich. She said that she was eager to try our goat's milk kefir, and asked if we'd like to contribute our story to her book of success stories, which of course we would!

And our proudest moment, when she actually wrote us an endorsement. It's on our website, and the way I feel at the moment, I may actually have it tattooed onto my bicep!

She said: 'I have tried the raw goat's milk and the goat's milk kefir probiotic from the Chuckling Goat, and they are wonderful! The taste and flavour are clean and pleasant, and I'm sure that any child or adult will like it. Many people can't tolerate cow's milk, so this is a perfect alternative. Goat's milk has a different protein profile, which makes it more compatible with human physiology and easier to digest. That's why in clinical practice children and adults generally tolerate goat's milk much better than cow's.'

Very proud moment, when we read that.

Rich and I have been pole-axed by the amount of work involved in running a business. What were we thinking??!

At the moment we have 16 goats, we're milking six, and feeding nine goat kids three times a day. On Tuesdays and Wednesdays, like today, Rich goes off to work at the harps and I'm here on my own. (They've asked him to come back for more days, but so far he's resolutely resisted. It's scary, because we're not making enough yet to replace his salary – but if we don't have his time and energy behind it all, we never will.)

That means I drop Joli and Benji at school at 8.30 a.m., then come back, feed all the goats, turn on the milking machine, wipe and milk the milkers, put fresh straw and hay out for all the goats, put extra milk into the bottles, feed the nine kids, who are now old enough to jump out of their pens, put their hooves up on my chest and fight each other – and me – for the milk!

Then the milk churn has to be hauled into the house (because the dairy's not finished yet), where the milk is filtered and bottled. Only one bright spot – because we've found a cheap source of milk bottles, we don't have to rinse, wash and disinfect recycled bottles. But the nine kid bottles still have to be washed three times a day.

And *then* any deliveries have to be made. And *then* maybe I sit down and have some breakfast. There're maybe two hours in the middle of the day to do computer chores, things like editing the final proofs of the book I'm co-writing with my boss, Peter Meyers, at Stand & Deliver. Or doing the soap labels. Or writing copy for the website. Or meeting with the computer guy to buy a reconditioned laptop that will actually run my business accounting software, since the bank neglected to tell me that it wouldn't work on my Apple Mac. And this after I'd already spent that whole day learning how to work with this particular software....

Then there's shopping, dinner prep, picking up the kids from school. And the whole two-hour milking-feeding routine has to happen again at night, after supper, before we fall into bed.

Goats, we say sometimes, looking at each other. Who'd have them?

It'll all get easier, we tell each other. It must. Little acorns. Little acorns...

26 May 2011

... and tonight, like every night, I emerge from the busy warmth and work and worry of the barn to my own private revelation stretched out over the hills down to the ocean, like the best bit of Narnia. Involuntarily, I put the buckets down, lean over the gate and stare, the wind from the Irish Sea fresh into my face.

Last night, smoky clouds, a silver sky over a silver sea. The night before, a bronzed mirror smeared with peach and turquoise. Tonight, a spill of liquid gold sideways onto all the backlit trees, marking each leaf with unbearable significance. In view of such a sight, I can forgive my enemies and bless everyone... well, nearly everyone.

No, then again, maybe not.

Not yet, anyway.

27 May 2011

A grey, tired morning. Deliveries to make today. Glenda still has a scabby udder, so her milk can't go into the bucket. And last night Buddug looked okay to begin with, but at the end her milk came out pink. It had already gone into the communal bucket, so the whole thing had to be tipped.

I have a magic back-fixer man and he tells me I shouldn't be lifting such heavy milk pails. I just laugh – what am I meant to do? Who's going to lift them if I don't? Rich woke up this morning with a stiff back as well – he cancelled his appointment yesterday because we ran out of time; I was finalizing the copy edits to the book, which had to go back to New York by that very afternoon, and then my boss Peter e-mailed at the last minute asking for help for a client of his, an American governor who needed assistance with writing the end of a speech. I thought the speech was terrific, very moving, and sat down to try to write the governor a proper conclusion, in the midst of everything else.

Rich came in to say that I should have told him in advance that I had work to do, so he could have got up earlier. I shouted at him that of course I always had bloody work to do, what did he think? So he went away and cancelled his physio appointment; they took him off the books, and now his back is out.

And on top of everything else, now I want harness goats... Margaret Shackles has two lovely identical little castrated males who'd look absolutely superb in harness, pulling Joli and Benji down the road on Barley Saturday. (This is the wonderful annual event in Cardigan, when they shut down the whole town, and run stallions down the high street.) Another fantasy, probably, that has nothing to do with the realities of feeding the little things for two years, getting them into harness, training them, trying to get them to cooperate.

I told Margaret Grant that I wanted them, and she laughed at me. 'Get your money coming in first,' she said. Rich said the same. But I still want them.

Made some of my Pecka Pickled Peppers this evening. Delicious. At least one thing went right today.

30 June 2011

The end of an absolutely horrendous week. We're back working at the Food Centre Wales again, trying to develop our kefir smoothies. The first time, of course, it went horribly wrong – 40 litres (70 pints) of milk down the drain.

Only slightly daunted, I returned, armed with 100 litres (175 pints) of milk this time. That's an awful lot of milk. Ten really big buckets full. We planned to run it through the high-tech pasteurizer that zips through 100 litres in 15 seconds, at a lower temperature. Hoping that the goaty flavour wouldn't be such a problem, if we did it like this.

The first day I went in, the pasteurizer popped a plate and started spraying green chemicals all over the floor. The pretty blonde technician clapped her hands to her cheeks in horror – not reassuring. So we siphoned all 100 litres out of the huge vat, back into the buckets I'd brought it in.

The buckets went back into the fridge, and I went home.

The next day I went in there was another problem with the machine. I went home again.

By then, the milk was on the verge of going off – and we were very close to losing all of it, plus the fees for the facility. Luckily, yesterday, the pasteurizer decided to bless us by working, and zipped through all 100 litres like a dream. A good thing, because I really wasn't looking forward to coming home and telling Rich that it had all been a waste. Two unsuccessful tries would shake his faith in the Food Centre – and I really can't see any other way for us to get approval to make our products.

So today, I went back to experiment with flavourings. There's a camel-choking amount of paperwork to do. One of the very kind and helpful employees at the Food Centre sat down with me at a long table, and went through the whole process for several hours. I dutifully took notes, but could feel my eyes glazing over with tiredness and disappointment that it was all going so badly.

Rich is back at the harps again, so I'm on my own with all the barn chores. And on Saturday it's the massive barn dance/barbecue that we have every year for our joint birthdays – Benji's and mine.

Benji's birthday is on Christmas Day, so we celebrate his half birthday in the summer, with a bouncy castle and an assault course. We set the bouncy castle up for the kids in the afternoon, and keep it up after dark for the adults, who play drinking games and have a whale of a time. This year we'll have Shetland pony rides as well, because my birthday present from Rich was a matching pair of Shetland ponies! But I'm just dreading the event this year, and wishing that the whole thing was over, and that I'd never agreed to do it in the first place.

When Rich asked me what I wanted for my birthday, I really couldn't think of anything. Clothes? Shoes? Handbags? Jewellery? It all seemed ridiculous, in my constant mud-and-goat-poo-stained state. My favourite place to shop is the army surplus store, where I can get cheap, warm and fleecy things to pull on before I go to the barn.

But then we went to visit some friends, Lou and Rob, and Lou had just got a Shetland pony. The tiny chestnut-coloured horse was adorable, with a quiff of blond mane between his ears. I felt a pang of acquisitive lust. Lou told me that her friend had two matched little Shetland stallions going spare, needing a good home. I immediately had visions of them pulling a cart, ribbons in their manes and tails; Benji in a cowboy outfit driving them down Cardigan high street. And suddenly, I knew exactly what I wanted for my birthday – Shetland ponies!

I got those harness goats, as well. They are gorgeous, with their shiny white and chestnut patterning, and worried wrinkled foreheads. Benji promptly dubbed them Roy and Trigger, as he's going through a Roy Rogers phase. We love them. But they're only tiny, and they won't be able to pull a cart for two years.

11 July 2011

Bright, hot and sunny day, with blue skies. My mother's 72nd birthday. I wish she was here with us today! Rich has gone out to begin to mow the hay – a momentous day, and a big risk. Today is Monday, and he has to gamble that the weather will be clear and sunny through to Friday. A near impossibility in Wales – and all the other factors have to be balanced as well.

The hay is so important for us – it's our main asset. We'd never be able to afford to buy in the amount of hay that we make, so it enables us to keep our animals through the winter. And we've never had so many – we're up to 22 goats now.

26 July 2011

Tomorrow is the Cardigan show and somehow – I'm still not sure how – we've been persuaded to enter and show our goats. I didn't want to. I was quite firm about that.

'We don't have time,' I told Rich and everyone else who asked. 'We're trying to launch this business. We're flat out. We simply haven't got time to prance around in white coats, competing in the show ring.'

But then Roz from the goat club called. 'Please,' she said. 'It's only me and Ian Grant entering goats at all this year. Without more entrants, they've threatened that next year they simply won't have a goat category.'

Rich and I talked about it – and it seemed clear that we needed to support the cause. It's important to us that the dwindling number of goat keepers in the area don't disappear altogether. No goat keepers means no billies, no nannies coming for our billies, no stock for us to buy or sell. We don't want that to happen – so we're going to have to do something about it.

And that something seems to be showing our goats.

So, Joli and I spent most of today scrubbing our white goats, trying futilely to remove the stains down their sides that come

Shann's Pecka Pickled Peppers

900g (2lb) sweet (bell) peppers

450g (1lb) apples

½ tsp salt

2 medium onions

1 tbsp lemon juice

¼ tsp fresh root ginger

115g (4oz) sultanas

225g (8oz) brown sugar

600ml (1 pint) white vinegar

1. Peel the onions and apples, and chop them up finely.

2. Place in a pan with the sugar, salt, vinegar, ginger and lemon juice and boil for 30 minutes.

3. Deseed the peppers and cut them into small cubes.

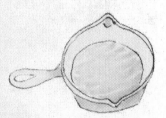

4. Add the peppers and the sultanas to the pan and simmer for 15 minutes.

5. Transfer the pickle to jars while it's still warm.

from the nasty habit they have of lying in their own poo – which they seem always to gravitate towards, despite the fact that we lay fresh straw every day.

The problem is that our great friends the Grants will be at the show tomorrow – they're the people who we've bought most of our white goats from, and they've shown for many years – and I can't stand the thought of showing up with our goats poorly turned out. It seems sloppy and ungrateful.

But the stains refused to shift – shampoo as we might. We tried the commercial white-horse shampoo from the farm co-op, tinted purple like the rinse that old ladies put on their hair. And at Joli's insistence, we also tried the cheaper combination of basic shampoo with a vinegar spray.

The horrible and expensive commercial product won hands down. The goat kid we washed with it gleamed an ethereal, show-winning, fluffy blue-white, while the homemade vinegar shampoo kid just looked damp and slightly yellow.

So. We washed the rest of the white goats with the expensive purple shampoo, and scrubbed them with the stain remover. But we still couldn't remove all the yellow stains on knees and flanks and brisket.

To top the problem, we all have to show wearing white coats. Ours arrived and were tried on for size, but they were wrinkled, from the packaging. This doesn't, on the face of it, seem like a huge problem. Just press them, you might say. But I'm a She-Who-Does-Not-Iron. It's always been a point of pride for me. If clothes need to be ironed, I send them to a dry cleaner, I used to say, back in the days when I owned *those* sorts of clothes.

These days my wardrobe consists of leggings that fit easily under my wellies-and-waterproof-rubber-trousers-combination that lurks always by the front door. And men's flannel shirts (short- or long-sleeved, depending on the season). And massive fleece jumpers, as warm and soft as possible. Nothing, but nothing, that needs ironing. Except, it seems, white goat-show coats.

Sigh. She-Who-Does-Not-Iron plugs in the iron and gets on with it...

24 August 2011

Well, we packed up 10 of our goats and went to the show. It was bright, hot and sunny. Two of the entrants were quarrelling about where to put the hurdles. Once they'd sorted out the details we put hurdles together to make our four pens, and released the goats into them. We gave them buckets of water, hay and branches to eat.

Children crowded around the pens, thrusting the branches into the goats' faces. We wandered idly until 1 p.m., when it was time for the judging. We put on our nicely ironed (!) white coats, dragged the goats into the ring and looked around at the other entrants – all of whom we knew – to find out what to do.

We lined up and held the goats facing forwards while they were examined by the judges, who handled their feet, checked their teeth and had a look at their udders. The goats apparently found this incredibly ticklish and ours – poorly trained, apparently! – had fits and tried to escape. Very embarrassing.

Then we led the goats around the ring, so that the judges could watch them walk, and then reversed direction and led them the other way. Then stood still again, while the judges had a last conference and placed us in order, and handed out rosettes, and shook our hands.

When the judging was all over, it turns out we won loads of rosettes, of which we're inordinately proud! It was hot, stressful and exhausting. Still, we came away wanting, for some strange reason, to do it again.

The idea behind these shows, I've decided, is that farming people don't get to go on vacations like other folks. You can't just hire in a pet sitter to look after 20 goats who need to be milked twice a day. But we still need some excuse for fun! So our outings are day outings, rather than two-week outings. The winters are harsh here, and most of the year everyone is on their own little isolated farm, struggling with the hardships that tending crops and animals bring.

But in the summer, the weather is milder, and everyone turns out to show what they've been working on so hard for the rest of the year. Breeding prize-winning sheep, making quilts, producing jam, sewing cushions, training horses – all the farming community brings out their best, to show off to one another. And that's a local summer fair. It was brilliant.

Lucky for us that we had that lovely day – because we've been having a horrific time since then. The bills keep flooding in – £500 to the vet for infectious disease testing, £200 per month for the feed. We've spent huge wads of cash doing up the barn, fitting out the dairy, painting and scrubbing and getting everything ready for the hygiene inspector. And now, at this moment, I have no money coming in.

The sales for milk are trickling – we're making around £50 per month. We've had to put off the approval day for the kefir, because the goats came down with a horrific virus that left their udders completely covered in oozing, scabby blisters. I milked Teasel by hand one day and came away feeling sick and nearly in tears, my hands covered with blood. It was like some horrible nightmare, but I just had to keep milking her, or she'd get sick with mastitis!

We'd wormed half the goats, and had to withdraw their milk for a week – in the meantime, they caught this virus. So we couldn't muster enough milk to take to the Food Centre Wales at Horeb. We've moved the date now – we won't be approved to sell the kefir until the first week of October.

So that only leaves the soap. And I'm terrified that I won't actually be able to sell it – or enough of it to make a difference. The thing is, we're to the edge now. We have the packaging and the labels. The soap is made and cured and sitting in the airing cupboard, ready to go. We're about to have the website ready to launch – and the massive bill for that to pay! So it's make or break time.

The whole idea suddenly seems ridiculous – whatever made us think that we could support ourselves in this way? I just want to go to bed and sleep, and sleep....

5 September 2011

Things are both a little better, and a little worse. We had a bit of a break with the hay – the weather abruptly turned warm and sunny, and we were able to mow and bale all of the hay but one field. So we should have enough for the coming winter.

But we are, abruptly, completely out of money. We spent our last £500 on three new goats and a load of straw – bedding for the winter. We need to get the goats up to a critical level so they can produce milk through the winter – if we're going to have any chance of keeping the business going until spring. So we cross our fingers, and hope.

30 October 2011

A relatively warm and sunny Sunday. Joli and Benji and I turned out to muck out some stalls in the goat barn – any dry day now, when the goats are outside, must be seized to do mucking out. Benji, age five, shovelled an entire stall's-worth of dirty straw into a neat heap, higher than his head. He worked like a full-grown man, all day, wrestling full wheelbarrows and slinging much with his full-size pitchfork – only the handle cut down to size for him.

And Joli got up earlier than anyone this morning and milked all 10 goats by herself, filtered the milk and made butter with her new electric butter churn – bought with money she earned from selling her first two goat kids. She amazes me – at age 12 she can skin a rabbit, turn it into a stew and accompany it with a loaf of homemade bread. She's also an A-star student, a fine flautist, reads incessantly and has biceps bigger than mine.

The farm has been brilliant for her. It has made her self-reliant, and unafraid of hard work. I'm very academic and tend towards the impractical, ivory-tower side of life, and Joli was much like me in that – but the farm has rounded her out, made her more pragmatic, taught her to handle all the difficulties of the real world. I wonder what kind of life she's going to choose for herself as she gets older.

And as for little Benji, he's become a complete mini-me of Rich. Rich has completely swept Benji up as his own – as has Taid, Rich's dad. Benji perches on the arm of Taid's chair like a little parrot in the evenings after supper, while Taid feeds him forbidden sweets, which they try to keep secret from me. (Ha! Fat chance – the all-seeing eye of Mother can always spot the evidence of random Haribos.)

But the real love affair here is between Rich and Benji. I often joke that Rich only took me on to get hold of Benji. They are certainly two peas in a pod – they sit on the squashy leather sofa, Benji tucked happily under Rich's arm, poring through tractor magazines and discussing the merits of 710s versus 810s, or why a Fordson Major is better than a David Brown.

Rich has bought Benji an entire toolkit – a proper one, not a toy version – and adds to it every Christmas and birthday. They come in together from the workshop – or man cave, as we call it – where Rich has a car pit and a treasure trove of man-junk. Aladdin chests full of curling wire, nuts and bolts, hammers and spark plugs, bits of engines from Land Rovers, the odd sit-on mower, clamps and wrenches and vices galore.

Accustomed to other men in my life who'd collect junk and never really use any of it, I used to think that Rich was just a hoarder, and that his man cave was just a conceit. But over time I've seen that he actually does use all these things – he can buy in a battered tractor and fix and weld and make new bits, until it actually goes again, and he can then use it around the farm or sell it on. Amazing. He's a bit of a wizard.

And so. gentle with it. Rich used to teach woodworking to schoolchildren, and he loves to have Benji trotting at his heels, banging nails into bits of wood and practising with his wrenches. Over time this relationship has grown, until now, Benji will actually anticipate Rich's needs, and like a fine nurse with a surgeon, will have the correct 7/8 drill bit (or whatever it's called!) to hand, just when Rich needs it.

The two of them come staggering in after long hours out in the workshop, black to the eyeballs with engine grease and grinning like twin fools. Rich says that if he can't have Benji (or his brother Rhys) to assist him out in the workshop, he'd rather be on his own, because it's faster. I certainly am no good at helping him – I just trip over things and stare stupidly at the jumble of tools, trying to work out which one he wants, until he sighs and gives up and gets it himself.

But Benji always knows, somehow, just what Rich needs.

And when Benji goes off to stay at his bio-dad's house, which he does on a regular basis, it's Rich, I think, who hurts the most. He's that little bit saddened, his spark a tiny bit quenched, until Benji comes back.

I miss Benj, when he goes. But Rich *grieves* for him.

It's a funny and complex thing, this creating of a blended family. There are four children here – I gave birth to two, and Rich fathered two. The way that we get around the split seams that generally keep something like this from working, is this:

1. Rich and I back each other, absolutely. Our first loyalty is always to one another, and we are indivisible on this. (Mind you, I can only afford this luxury because I can trust

completely in Rich's innate kindliness – he'd take a bullet for any of my children, or his, so I need never fear for them.) Any disagreement we have on how to handle the kids, we discuss in private. But in public, we're always a unit. This has ensured that the kids aren't able to get in and drive a wedge between us, which is always a kid's tendency, isn't it?

2. We try our level best to make sure everything is equal and fair. Everyone gets the same, and genetics don't factor into it. Taid is brilliant about this – he has embraced all the kids, and treats Joli and Benji just the same as his genetic grandchildren. He gives everyone the same thing for Christmas, and for birthdays. He's welcomed us into his home with more grace than I ever would have imagined or expected.

My own father, to my eternal grief and shame, seems completely uninterested in entering this sort of experience. He's only concerned with his own genetic grandchildren, and so I feel pity for him, as he's shut himself out of a world of loving and happy connections. Such a sad thing – and such a deep, ongoing loss for him.

But the rest of us know a true secret – that families are not born, but *made*. Made with determination and loyalty and fierce resolve. It's a choice, and a discipline. It's a practice. It's a path that you walk.

Families don't have to be genetically related. Far from it. Families are groups of people who *choose* to love each other. They can come in all shapes and colours and sizes, and be made up of all sorts of unlikely individuals. Connection is connection – and it's always golden.

Anyhow, back on the farm we loaded the wheelbarrows full of muck into the tipping trailer, which Rich will later drive into the field with the big blue tractor, and empty onto the muck heap. There it'll rot down until it's ready to be spread back onto the fields.

The two children were in the barn, forking the dirty straw into the wheelbarrows. Then they rolled the barrows out, and Joli and I lifted each wheelbarrow up and turned it upside down into the tipping trailer. Then they went back for another load, and I forked the straw towards the back of the trailer to make space for the next load, trampling it underfoot to pack it down.

There was one moment, when I paused for breath on top of the growing mountain of straw, and looked out towards the sea. The sun was warm and bright on my shoulders, spreading the mountains with sherbet colours – peach and mango and russet brown. The landscape was, abruptly, almost unbearably near and tender – personal, like a message from someone I'd loved long ago. I suddenly felt completely happy. The shovelling, the manual labour, leaves my mind calm and clear, emptied. Dirty stalls, clean mind.

On another note, we've been completely out of money for almost two months. And oddly, it's been a freeing thing. We've cut our grocery bills by about 90 per cent. We've bought nothing that we could make. Our shopping list looks like something from the pioneer days – sugar, flour, oil, tea, bacon. I went to the farmers' market and bought bags of potatoes and carrots, plus boxes of plums to make jam and chutney.

Joli's been making butter for us in her new electric butter churn, whipping the milk until the grains form and then smoothing and working the results with a wooden paddle until she has delicious, pure white butter.

We worked our way through the unused tins of food in the kitchen cabinet. And somehow, we found, we were eating better than we ever had. I made goat's cheese on a regular basis, and we kept the bread machine humming every day. If we got a craving for sweets, we made oatmeal cookies. We threw a party and cooked everything from scratch.

Somehow, having no money to spend at the shop made us creative, and clever. The gift of poverty, perhaps.

2 December 2011

First frost today, and the hills and hedges are iced with the faintest silver, reflecting the palest pinks, smoky lavenders and baby blues of the sky… I love this time of year in Wales; in the early morning, when the icy mists hang over the icy fields, and everything is coloured with the most delicate pastels.

On the way to school, Benji said, 'It looks sad when all the hedges have lost their leaves, doesn't it, like they've died?'

'But what's really true?' I said.

'They're only sleeping,' he said triumphantly. 'And they'll come back in the spring.'

And that, I figure, is just about all I need to know.

Fate must have overheard me boasting to my mother that I wasn't satisfied with the book *Chop Wood, Carry Water: A Guide to Finding Spiritual Fulfillment in Everyday Life*, and that I planned to write my own version. Fine words, spoken from the depths of a comfy chair, holding a glass of sherry. A very different thing on a cold, bright, wintry morning when everything is frozen hard as bone and I have to actually carry water, because all the water buckets are full of ice.

So, as I filled the yellow bucket from the one remaining unfrozen tap, I tried to remember why it was that I ever thought this whole process of carrying water was worthwhile and interesting. I decided to think of it as research for the book. The first thing that occurred to me as I carried water is that carrying water is a pain in the arse! It's heavy, it's awkward, and it constantly slops onto your leg as you walk.

The second thought, following close on the first, is that you'd only carry water if you had to. It's not one of those things that you do for fun. Carry a bouquet of flowers, maybe... carry a lace handkerchief, carry a cuddly toy. But you don't carry water for a laugh.

You carry water because if you don't, something will die. You carry water in the desert, where it's hot and dry, because you don't have water where you live. You carry water to animals when it's cold and frozen, because they'll perish if you don't. It's always a matter of life and death to carry water – as urgent as anything could possibly be.

But it's also slow. Most urgent things can be accomplished quickly. But carrying water is something that you necessarily do at a plodding pace. Try to rush, and it spills everywhere and you arrive at your destination with cold, wet legs and an empty bucket.

And then, abruptly, my mind clears, and is filled with stillness. There's no point in railing at the ice, the bucket or the thirsty animals. There's no-one to blame, and no-one to argue with. There's only the clear, bright path from the tap to the barn, the frozen air, the weight of the bucket, the endless blue sky and the silence, broken only by a single dog barking somewhere over the mountain....

When Rich asked me what I wanted for Christmas, all I could think of was two more goats. I know, kind of crazy!

After all, what else would a girl want? I honestly couldn't imagine. I've never been in the position before where my avocation is the same as my vocation – where my passion is also the way that I make my living. It's an eye-opener, I must say. We do eat, breathe, sleep and dream goats – and so that's what I asked for as my Christmas present. Two more goats.

Not just any goats, though. Looking ahead and poring over the big wall calendar, we could see that there was going to be a long dry period in February. Most of the goats would be dried off, as they have to rest for two months before kidding. And where would all our milk come from then?

I began to panic about the dry spell. Our infant business, less than a year old, depends on our being able to supply our customers with goat's milk whenever they want it. So the goats

I wanted were ones due to kid in January, that would be ready to milk in February, guaranteeing us an ongoing milk supply.

We found some that fitted the bill and had driven to England to collect them just before Christmas, a five-hour drive each way. They were delicate as deer, young and white, little more than goatlings. But they were beautiful, they were in kid, and they were mine. Merry Christmas!

We watched the new goats grow bigger and rounder day by day, unsure as to when they would kid. They came from a large commercial herd, where the due date of each individual goat wasn't kept.

Then one day Joli came racing into the house. 'Kidding, kidding!' she gasped out. I was already pulling on my wellies and waterproof trousers, shouting for Rich: 'Kidding!' I raced out behind Joli, pulling off my wedding ring. I cursed when I realized that I hadn't cut my nails – usually, during kidding season I always keep them extra-short, just in case.

When we got to the stall, the first goat, Wandi, was bleating and looking confused. Out of her backside protruded a swollen, dead-looking goat kid head – just the head, nothing else. The eyes were closed, the tongue protruding. Joli and I stopped, shocked.

Rich pounded in just after us and let himself into the stall.

'Is it dead?' I asked.

'Goodness knows how long it's been stuck here,' he said and felt the head. 'The head is cold, anyway.'

I shivered and gripped my elbows, but after three years on the farm I've seen some amazing things. Life is powerful and not to be denied – many a lamb that looks dead to begin with can revive and be skipping around a day later.

Rich knelt down and started to explore the goat's back end. 'Both legs back,' he announced. A goat kid ideally comes into the world headfirst, like a diver, two tiny cloven hooves tucked neatly under its chin. Once the head and the two front legs emerge, the rest of the body follows.

But on this one, both legs were back, rotating the shoulders into a wide blocking position, and only the head had come through. Left on its own, it would die. If it hadn't already.

I took a deep breath and let myself into the stall to stand beside Rich. He was cursing softly, trying to wedge himself into the small space.

'I can't get to it,' he said.

'Let me,' I said. 'My hands are smaller.' It's not something I would have said when I first arrived on the farm. Then, I panicked when Rich asked me to help. It seemed an unbearably heavy burden to take on – the responsibility for an animal's birth resting on me. What if I did something wrong? What if I hurt it? What if it died, and it was all my fault? How would I know what to do?

I have, since then, taken a lambing class (which seemed remarkably uninformative) and watched Rich 'pulling' lambs. But none of this seems to really help in the moment when something needs doing. Then, everything is stark and spot-lit and very clear.

There were only the five of us here – Rich, Joli, me, the goat and her kid's head, with its dead-looking tongue sticking out of one side of its mouth. Rich's hands were too big. I couldn't ask Joli, at age 13, to do what I wouldn't do myself. Wandi the goat couldn't help herself. And by the time anyone else showed up, the kid would be dead.

And anyway, suddenly I could see inside my head what needed to be done. I could picture the kid, with its front legs trailing back behind it. I could imagine just how it looked, inside that dark womb.

Rich moved aside and let me kneel down behind the goat.

'I forgot the lube gel,' I said.

'Never mind,' he replied. 'We haven't got time.'

I worked my hand around the cold kid's head, around the tightly stretched rim of the goat's birth opening. I closed my eyes, the better to pay attention to the picture that was in my head. I followed the kid's neck down – there was its shoulder, there was its leg, and yes, the foot, with the small, soft hoof on the end. I just needed to cup my hand around the hoof – there – and bring it up.

'Yes!' said Rich. 'That's it!'

'Other foot?' I said.

'No, it can come with one foot out. Now pull.'

I looked for a place to pull. The head? The neck? The leg? And somehow I was pulling, and the goat kid was sliding out, in a long, steady rush. It lay on the straw, looking extraordinarily lifeless.

I grabbed a towel and started rubbing it gently. 'Come on, little one,' I said. 'Breathe.' It took a gasp, and then there was a long pause. Then another gasping, rattling breath. Its head was swollen from the long time outside the womb, making it disproportionately large compared to the body.

Rich checked between the kid's long legs. 'A boy,' he said. We all groaned in unison. For us, a male kid is not a reason to rejoice. We can't keep all the males, or we'd soon be overrun.

Newborn kids are left with their mothers for four days, nursing the thick, creamy colostrum that their mothers produce. That helps the mother's milk come in properly, and the kids get what they need from the colostrum, which is rich in vitamins and antibodies.

On day four, the female goat kids are taken away from their mothers to be de-horned at the vet's. When they come back they smell strange – of the vet's office and the bright blue spray that decorates the spot where the horn buds used to be – and they're hungry. A perfect time to wean them onto the bottle, and separate them from their mothers.

The mothers get turned into the milkers' pen, where they club around with their other milker pals – goats are, first and last, social animals – and are stroked, fussed over, fed and milked morning and night. The kids are bottle-fed five times a day at first, then four, then three, for about nine weeks.

Bottle-feeding gives us a chance to handle the kids, so that they're tame and friendly and imprinted on human beings. This is important because a goat that can't be easily handled by humans is nearly impossible to milk. A goat kid raised only by its mother can be as shy and wild as a wood deer. So the system works for everyone.

With luck, a female kid will grow into a replacement milker, to be kept or sold. If we decide to keep her, we enter a relationship that'll last the whole of her life. We'll see her and feed her, stroke and milk her every day, twice a day.

We'll come to know her intimately: know her quirks and foibles, know how much she eats and what treats she prefers; whether or not she kicks; whether she sheds. When she's old enough we'll mate her to the billy, and watch her bear her own offspring, generation upon generation. Or we'll sell her, for a handsome fee, to someone who values her pedigree and will treasure her as a productive milker.

The tough calculus of the farm means that you only need one male for every 20 or so females – males are harder to find places for. But I work over this one, rubbing him with the towel, talking to him, trying to get his body going. Slowly, his breathing becomes more regular. His mother prods him with her nose, licking him. His gasping breaths steady, his eyes flicker open. Amazingly, it looks as though he'll survive.

We put in fresh straw and a bucket of warm water and leave them for the night.

And then, some good luck for the newborn male! Margaret and Ian Grant phone and say that they want the little male goat to stand stud at their farm. They've been researching his pedigree, and have come to the conclusion that his bloodlines are good enough to warrant taking him on. They'll take him to foster, and he'll serve their goats as soon as he's old enough. Then he can come back to us, and serve our goats. Because his mother and father both came from the outside, he's a fresh bloodline.

I go to bed that night rejoicing, my heart ridiculously light. If the new little male is going to be an honoured stud goat, then he deserves a proper name! We decide to call him Hoffnant Boston. Hoffnant because that's our herd name – from Brynhoffnant, the stream that runs by our house. And Boston, because we name our goats after American place names, to honour my American bit of the equation.

Hoffnant Boston. It has a certain ring.

In the morning we all rush out to see how Boston is doing. He's up – he's alive! Staggering around, looking a big bleary, but definitely alive, gaining and nursing. A victory...

12 March 2012

We were on TV! Very exciting. The team from Heno, the Welsh language programme, came out and filmed a sequence about us that aired tonight on S4C – a beautifully cut piece that had the goats, the milking, the bottling, Benji and the soaps. It was so strange, watching ourselves out with the goats, rambling down the hillside. I didn't talk at all, as I still can't speak Welsh – but Rich and Benji carried the day. I was tremendously, fiercely proud of our little business and our Hoffnant herd.

14 March 2012

The other end of the equation to the triumphant birth of Hoffnant Boston: we just had to send Paris away – wise, kind, dignified old Paris, the Anglo-Nubian stud male. He was balding on his back, and had an abscess on his cheek. But he looked at us with large, liquid eyes, and there was intelligence there. I loved him, loved passing his stall and feeding him a treat. But his time had come, and he was old and ill.

Benji and I took out a banana skin to give him, his favourite treat, and stroked him. We watched as the horrible little man in the dark hat loaded him into the van. He jumped so willingly, so trustingly. Then we came inside and sat in the big armchair with our arms wrapped around each other, and cried. Poor Paris. Sometimes farming breaks my heart....

16 March 2012

Rich has just driven off to the hospital.

We'd kept his ulcerative colitis in remission for a long time – 14 months – with the goat's milk kefir and meat broths, but then it all started up again. He tried steroids, which didn't seem to work, and went back to the doctor, who has run out of solutions. It seems to me that at the end of this road is the dark, looming prospect of an operation and I'm very nervous about it.

Just yesterday, we pulled out Dr Campbell-McBride's book and looked again at the diet. What she recommends for someone in an extreme situation – which, let's face it, is where Rich is now – is a diet with no fibre at all. Just meat broth and probiotics, until the lining of the gut heals and things calm down.

We decided to do it together – I would eat whatever Rich did, to keep him company. I made a huge vat of lamb broth. I ate it with him this morning, and it was delicious – lightly salted, warm and soothing. We drank it out of mugs, and followed it with some of our homemade goat's milk kefir.

Then the hospital called – a bed had become available, and they wanted him in right away. Why, we're not sure; they'll do some tests, the secretary said vaguely. Maybe give him some more infliximab – a drug that worked for him once, long ago, and then stopped working.

I was on my way to town to drop off a goat kid at the vet for dehorning, and make some milk deliveries, when Rich phoned to say that he'd be going into hospital. More than anything, I wanted to go with him. I've always been with him for his hospital visits. Just an instinctive, primal thing. If he's there, I want to be there with him.

But I can't this time. There are goats to be milked, and one due to kid any moment. The sheep are lambing, and need to be fed and watered and given hay. Joli and her friend need to be picked up from school, and the goat kid needs to be collected from the vet. Joli and Benji, and the increasingly frail Taid, need to be fed their supper, *and* it's fish and chips night.

Children and animals and old people all need tending, and there's only me to do it. The farm and its duties descend on me like a hammer blow – I have to stay here, when all I want is to be with Rich.

As good as it gets! Joli and I take a break to soak up some 'goat love'.

This handsome fellow, Dexter, was one we had before we decided no horns allowed...

Who says goats don't belong inside?

My Rich, doing his goat magic...

Benji and his beloved Buddug. This is the picture he had on his birthday cake.

Benji, the little goat herd. He gets paid for his barn work, and he earns it.

A good day for Chuckling Goat at Cardigan Show!

Feeding Lola when she was just a kid... and now we're about to welcome her great-granddaughters!

Rich and his right-hand man, Benji.

My beloved Teasel and me.
(Janet Baxter)

*Home on the farm
– this is the dairy.*

*This is why I get so enraged when I
see goats in sheds their whole lives,
never allowed to see the light of day or
feel the sun on their backs. Don't tell me
these animals don't have feelings! This is Silica
and Dime, having a loving moment. (Janet Baxter)*

The family on the farm. Left to right:
Joli, Elly, me, Ceris, Rich and Benji.

Winter on the farmyard.

Patsy wants a scratch
behind the ears.

The farm gang. Clockwise from top left: me, Joli, Elly, Benji, Ceris.

This is Rado (short for Hoffnant Colorado) daughter of Valentine, and granddaughter of Marmite. (Janet Baxter)

Two of the Nut Brown Maidens, as we call them – Lola's daughters. Chattanooga and Cadillac – Chatty and Caddy for short. (Janet Baxter)

Chuckling Goats love the sun! *(Janet Baxter)*

*Taid – our cherished patriarch.
His chair is still empty.*

*Skin cream-
making at our
not-so-corporate
headquarters! This
is the farmhouse
kitchen table where
it all happens...*

The unsinkable Mrs Jones.

My happy ending.

Natural healing power from Chuckling Goat – our award-winning range of kefir and skincare products. (Janet Baxter)

I had an interesting experience yesterday, as I struggled to adjust to doing the work of two people, on my own. I found that the ritual and the routines of the farm, far from weighing me down, actually supported and sustained me. The milking has its own routine, and once you enter the beginning, it carries you through it, like a dance, under its own power.

Switch on the water heater, turn on the radio, hook up the milk machine, put the food into bowls, put the first goat up on the stand – the beat of the milking machine, the music on the radio, the contented noises of the goats as they wolf down their cake. These things are familiar, and sustaining. Hay, straw and water the goats. Every morning, every night. It doesn't need thought; it just needs doing. It's comforting.

And as it was a Friday, it was fish and chips night – as always. When we were ploughing every penny into the business, and couldn't afford to go out any more, Friday remained fish and chips night. We bought the fish from the shop, and Rich made homemade chips in the deep fat fryer.

And yesterday, though Rich wasn't there to make the chips, it was still fish and chips night. I bought the chips from the Bowens, and Ceris reheated them in the oven. The tradition carried me along.

One of the goats kidded last night – among the things that I've been worried would happen while Rich is away. But it was easy – I walked in, and the kid was already standing, white fur fluffed up, mother licking it contently. A girl! Big, and strong and healthy. Couldn't be better.

I sprayed her umbilical cord with iodine, and squirted some Kick Start into her mouth, milked out the mother goat and gave the colostrum to the baby in a bottle. She took it, eagerly. Liliwen, the mother, has a gammy foot that we've been waiting to treat, not wanting to hassle her while she was heavily pregnant.

She kept kicking the kid away when it came too near the painful foot. So we separated out the kid, put it in the crèche with the other kids, on their nice clean straw under the heat lamp. And we got on with the milking because it was time to milk.

On the farm, there are times to do everything. And even in crisis, the wheel moves on, demanding that I move with it. So I can surrender to it, and it carries me along, despite worrying about Rich in hospital.

I've discovered something else, as well. Exhaustion is mental. I don't mean that it's all in my mind, and doesn't really exist. Exhaustion is a real thing, no doubt about it! What I mean is that, for me, exhaustion is rarely physical. It's rare that I'm doing something that taxes my body to the physical breaking point. Although on the farm that happens too... but it never used to in the city, and I experienced exhaustion so many times there.

What I mean is that exhaustion for me comes from mentally racing ahead, from being overwhelmed by how much there is to do. Looking over the various mountains that have to be climbed during the day, and feeling worn out before I begin. Whereas, of course, all those tasks never have to be done at once. Only one thing at a time has to be done.

Under crisis, I've decided, I need to shrink my focus. The more intense the crisis, the smaller the focus. When things are really bad, I can focus just on the next thing I have to do. That much, surely, is do-able.

It's not hard to milk. It's not too difficult to eat breakfast. Easy, in fact. Pips, as Benji would say. It's not a strain to put the dishes in the dishwasher. It's not difficult to get in the car and drive to Swansea, to see Rich in hospital.

If I stay in the moment, simply moving through each second as it arises, I'm fine. It's battering myself mentally against the *idea* of everything I have to do that causes the sensation of exhaustion. One foot in front of the other… steadily, evenly. And if it gets worse than that, I can always shift the focus again. Even smaller. Just down to the next breath. Breathing in… breathing out…

22 March 2012

I've been running the farm on my own now for six days, while Rich is in hospital. On the first night, Joli came in to tell me that a sheep had died. There was a long moment when I wondered why she was telling me – what was I supposed to do about it? Then I realized that I'd have to do something and that if I didn't, no-one would. It would just stay there and rot, I suppose. In the middle of the pen of other sheep, who are busy lambing. That obviously wasn't a good idea.

What does one do with a dead sheep? Rich always sorts these things out – he spares me as much of the unpleasantness as he can. But he wasn't here to spare me now. I was going to have to work it out.

I wanted to spare Joli if I could, and do it myself, so I went up to investigate. Pulled the string to turn on the light in the big, cavernous barn. The sheep milled around in the open pen – all except one. It was lying there stiffly. Definitely dead.

I went over to it and grabbed its fleece, thinking that perhaps I could drag it out of the pen. Two handfuls of fleece came away in my hands. I dropped them and backed away. This wasn't going to be as easy as I'd thought – and I wasn't going to be able to spare Joli. I was going to need her help. Ceris and Elly are away at school, and we're the only ones here to get the job done.

We milked and got the animals bedded for the night, then came in and had supper. Music and candles on the table every night, as usual. It helps me, to keep these things going. Gives me an illusion of control and sanity. I looked at Joli after supper. Her lovely face gazed back, serene and level-eyed. 'We've got to do that dead sheep,' I said apologetically. 'I know,' she said.

We walked out to the barn together, arm in arm. I got a wheelbarrow, and we wheeled it through the dark, back up to the barn.

'My friends are on Facebook right now,' Joli said reflectively. 'Or doing internet shopping.' This struck us, for some reason, as being extremely funny, and we giggled a bit hysterically.

Together we managed to lever the dead sheep into the wheelbarrow and forced the wheelbarrow up the steep slope, opened the big padlocked gate and tipped the body out onto the flat space, ready for the knacker man to pick up.

We debated for a while what to cover it with, settling finally on a big dumpy bag that the goat food comes in. We covered the body and weighted it down with stones. When I looked down, there was a leg poking gruesomely out of the white covering. I pushed it back in and pulled the bag over further to cover it.

'I don't know how people in the Mafia do it,' I mused. 'Dealing with dead bodies is hard work.' Amazing what you can do when you have to cope… I keep reaching down further and further to find reserves.

The worst day of being on my own was yesterday. I dropped Benji off at school and came back to milk the goats. But first I had to send off an order for goat's milk kefir, which meant that I had to contact FedEx – we've just started using them to ship out our milk orders. But the computer wasn't printing the label properly, so I had to contact the office. He wanted me to talk to the IT bloke to sort it out, but I told him I couldn't because I had to milk the goats. I hand wrote the label and left it for the delivery man to pick up.

Then I started out to milk, but Taid told me that I was needed up in the sheep barn for a new lamb. When I got there, I found that one of the sheep had given birth to a tiny, yellow lamb that was struggling feebly on its own. No-one had licked it or fed it. I looked accusingly at all the sheep, ranged on the other side of the barn. 'Okay, whose is it?' I said. They all looked back at me guiltily, but no-one confessed.

I picked up the baby, sprayed its belly button with iodine, forced some Kick Start down its throat. I trudged back to the house, made up a bottle of powdered colostrum and warm water and firmly fed it some from a bottle. In the meantime, Taid identified the sheep he thought was the mother. We caught her and penned her up, but when I reached under her thick, dirty fleece to check her udders, they were completely flat – no milk at all.

I sighed – looks like I'm mum to yet another lamb. Just what I don't need at the moment. I carried the new lamb down to the crèche, where we have three goat kids and one lamb snuggled in a small wooden pen under a heat lamp. I put it in with the other babies and finally started to milk – at 11 a.m. Milking takes two hours, but I had to stop at 12:30 to do some coaching on the computer. I did three sessions, back to back.

I worked right up until it was time to stop, and just managed to get the milk filtered and in the freezer – I didn't have time to give the goats extra hay, or turn them out, or give the kids their early afternoon feed, or check on the new lamb, or give it another feed.

I thought, *the lamb might die. I need to feed it.* But I also had to get on my conference call. The executives at Cisco were waiting, and they didn't know or care about my new orphan lamb charge. I had to be in two places, and I couldn't.

I went in and fired up the computer, still smelling of afterbirth from where I'd cradled the lamb. We needed the money that I'd make from these sessions, and I needed to keep my job. If I missed the session, my credibility with the company would be destroyed, and no excuse would be good enough. The lamb would have to take its chances. But leaving the animals unfed was like a physical pain – I hated it.

As soon as the session was over I called Joli (who had just come home from school) and we raced out to the barn together. She gave the goats hay and water, while I fed the kids. Everyone had survived.

Joli washed out the milking machine, and I went inside and sat down for five minutes, staring out the window. It was the first time, I realized, that I'd sat down all day. I rested there quietly and drank one glass of sherry. Then I heaved myself out of the chair and went to do the evening milking.

I phoned Rich to report on what was happening. He's now scheduled for emergency surgery on 6 April. He'll be home for two weeks first, and then will go back in for the operation.

Two weeks of having him home – and then another week in hospital. This time, we'll be better prepared. I can call friends, organize milking rotas. Ask the Grants to take the goat kids for the week. Joli can milk at night, and I'll ask people to come over and help. I have two weeks to make double portions of things and put them in the freezer. We can do this. We have to do this. We have no choice.

24 March 2012

Brilliantly sunny this morning – funny how that makes everything feel more cheerful! Rich is back from hospital for two weeks. It's bliss to have him home. I picked him up on Thursday, and was shocked to see how pale and shaky he was, with grey shadows under his eyes. They had him on massive doses of steroids, which didn't help at all, but now he has to withdraw from them, which is going to make him feel even worse.

On Rich's first evening, we sat outside. We let out the three goat kids and the two orphan lambs we're bottle-feeding, and Joli and Benji played with them in the grassy area where the swings are. We perched on the steps leading down to the swing set and turned our faces up to the slanting sun, which painted everything gold. We could see out over the bowl of our valley to the sea, blue and mysterious, in the distance.

We never do this, normally. Rich, when he's well, is constantly in action. He hates the idea of drinking tea because he can't tolerate the time it takes to make it. But this time he sat contently on the step, looking out. A gift, this beautiful half-hour; a gift out of the illness. I will take this and squeeze it for whatever it has to offer.

The weather today is amazing – warm and balmy – the first proper day of spring. Air like shandy: fizzy and sweet and making everyone slightly drunk on sun. Green grass shining. That's a lovely thing about Wales, it's so damp that when the sun does come out, everything gleams as if freshly scrubbed! Joli's lying on her stomach in the field by the swings, reading, with the three goat kids and two lambs curled up next to her in the sun. I'm going to make lavender and mint and lemon soap in my big pan on the stove. Bliss...

Later – Joli's doing homework at one end of the kitchen table, while I make soap at the other. Ceris, home on a break from university, is doing coursework in her room. The girls have agreed to meet for a break and a coffee at 3 p.m. But when it's time for a break, Rich sends Joli out to look at the sheep, who are still in the middle of lambing. Joli comes back to report that Mansel, her pet lamb from last year who's a grown-up sheep now, is lambing and has two back feet sticking out.

I wonder briefly, when did Joli learn to tell the back feet from the front? It's not easy to tell the difference – I always struggle to remember which way up they point. When all you can see of the lamb being born is its hooves, it's critical to know if they're front or back. If they're back hooves, you've got to reach in and make sure the bony little tail is smoothed down, or it'll rip the mother as you pull it out.

And you can't hesitate – once you start to pull, the umbilical cord breaks, and with its head in the birth canal, the lamb will suffocate. Front hooves are easier because that's the way the lamb is intended to be born. Joli will grow up knowing these things, while I had to learn them, piece by piece.

I asked if they needed me outside, but Rich said they didn't, so Joli went out with him, and I carried on making soap. We have our first big trade order due to go out this week, and I've a horrible, nagging fear that something will go wrong. I'll come up short of soap somehow at the last minute – stupid, but I haven't had a minute until now to actually make any soap. And I'll be damned if I let the business go now, when we've worked so hard for the past year to get it going.

We've just now been contacted by Prince Charles's company, Cambrian Mountain Initiative, to make soap for them. We're teetering on the edge of what could be success, and I refuse to pop it all now, like taking a pin to a balloon. We must manage to keep it going while Rich is in hospital – somehow.

Joli just came in through the front porch, where Ceris has been sunning herself, curled up like a cat on the bench, and asked for some Depocillin (a penicillin jab we keep in the fridge to dose the sheep and goats when something goes wrong). She was covered in blood up to her elbows.

'Bad?' I asked as I took the bottle from the fridge, broke open a new syringe packet, attached a sterile needle and deftly drew a dose of the thick white liquid into the syringe. (*When did I get good at this?* I wondered.)

My mother phoned earlier for an update. I told her, because I thought I should, that Rich's colostomy is an emergency one and that there's a risk of his colon perforating in the meantime. A small risk, but a risk nonetheless. My mother asked me about it again, later in the conversation.

'I don't want to talk about it,' I said. 'It's not going to happen, and I don't want to discuss it.'

I don't want to think, during this brief, fragile period of having Rich at home before he goes back to hospital, how fragile it all really is.

25 March 2012

Last night, Rich said, 'What's happening to you? When I look at you, you're glowing.'

I asked him what he meant, and he said, 'You eat like I used to, these days. Quickly, and loads of food. And it just seems like you're running things. When I used to come to the barn, and you were milking, you'd stop, as if you had all day. Now, you're in a rhythm. You just get on with things. You talk to me, but you don't stop. And you don't seem tired – you seem energized.'

I thought about what he'd said, and it's true. I do feel stronger, more energized. Like when you start doing something new, and the muscles ache and pang, and finally they give in and start getting stronger. It's as if I've found a whole new gear from which to operate. I think the truth is that I've finally put my arms around this farm.

I loved it before, but it wasn't mine. Rich was always there, strong and tall as a wall – experienced, knowledgeable. If I felt tired or didn't want to do something, all I had to do was complain, and he'd take care of it. Like moving into adulthood – now it's my responsibility. And that knowledge has released some new strength in me.

And not just me – yesterday I stopped at the army surplus shop and bought proper grown-up green waterproof trousers for Joli, and a wooden-handled knife like mine. We use the knives for cutting open bales of hay and haylage, and she was always asking to borrow mine. I handed them over to her ceremonially, telling her that she'd earned them, which she has. She was inordinately pleased.

It's funny, the farm has made her very tough, and unfussy. She came back into the house yesterday with lamb poo down the front of her T-shirt, and laughed as she told me the story: 'The lamb had poo on it; the mother licked the lamb and then licked me. And I didn't want to move, because I was feeding the lamb, and because the mother was bonding with me.'

She looked down at her stained T-shirt. 'No point in changing this now. I'm only going back out. Have you got a rubber band?' I gave her one, and she matter-of-factly tied her T-shirt up so that the poo was out of the way. It looked very fetching.

'There we go,' she said. 'All sorted.' And she went back out to the barn.

Today was another stunning day! Sunny and warm... Joli and I milked. She fed the babies (current count – three goat kids, two orphan lambs and two lamb twins still with their mother, but she's not producing enough milk). That's seven baby bottles that need to be used, washed and refilled, three times daily.

Rhys came over to help drive in fence posts, where the goats had broken the fence down and got into the goose run. Rich is looking so ill... pale green, with great grey shadows under his eyes. He's quickly out of breath. And he's so used to forcing himself on, it's difficult to make him sit down and rest. It frightens me more than I can say when I tell him to put his feet up, and he does, without complaint.

Joli and I cut up all the soap batches I made yesterday, and she labelled and packaged them. Today is Sunday – the day of rest! Funny... the work never stops on the farm. The goats don't take the weekends off, and neither do the farmers. Tomorrow I must grudgingly send Joli back to school – she loves packaging the soap, and it's fun to sit around the table, chatting and listening to music, while we slide the beautiful-smelling bars into their crisp canvas bags, tying on the coloured labels.

Now I have to make more soap, strain the goat's milk kefir and bottle it, and get that all done and the table cleared off before it's time for the evening meal. Our big, cheerful farmhouse kitchen is like a factory. The table is constantly being covered with projects and then cleared, like a massive tide coming in and out.

But every night, without fail, all the projects are put away, the candles set out and the music put on. We eat fresh, homemade bread and huge pots of stew, our own cheese and jams and chutneys. I love suppertime... I love the fact that the family is all together in one place, and we have this moment of peace and beauty to buoy us up.

Whatever else is happening outside, it seems critically important that we put on the music, light the candles and sit down together. It's the hub that keeps the crazy spokes of the wheel in place, gathered together at the centre.

26 March 2012

Feeling completely overwhelmed today. We were up until 11:30 p.m. last night, getting colostrum down two lambs that had just been born. Joli went out to feed the babies and was so long coming in that Rich went out after her. We have walkie-talkies so that we can communicate between the barn and the house, but they're not working at the moment – one of the many things on my long list to replace.

When Rich went out, he found Joli with two new baby lambs, whose mother was just staring at them dopily, trying to work out what they were. Rich came back in and mixed up powdered colostrum and went back out to try to feed it to them. He came in half an hour later, frustrated. They had only taken a little bit.

I re-warmed what was left in the bottle, which had grown stone-cold, and went out again. He came with me. It was a clear, mild night, bright with stars. I always resent going out so late, when sensible people are in watching TV, but taking a deep breath of the sweet night air and looking up at the stars always makes me glad to be outside again.

Anyway, I was able to coax most of the rest of the colostrum down the two lambs. One took it eagerly. The other, still wet with afterbirth, had to have his head jiggled, and the bottle squeezed to get it down him. Or her. I didn't check. That late at night, I didn't care.

Rich had a pretty good night but a rough morning, so I've left him in bed to sleep. Joli is still in her room – hasn't done the morning shift of feeding the babies. Fair enough, she worked like a hero all weekend. So now I've got to get Benji fed and off to school, and feed seven babies – or nine, counting the two from last night.

And that's before I even start the shift of milking and barn work, which has to be completed before I sit down to any paperwork or ordering. Or FedEx, for the deliveries, or calling the stockists to tell them we're closing down the business while Rich is in hospital. The only way I'm going to get through this day is to practise my new skills, faithfully. They're not theoretical – they're about survival.

So. Let's see. What have I learned? Don't get overwhelmed. Don't think about everything that needs doing. Just do the thing that's right in front of me, at the farm pace that means you move slowly and inevitably towards something. Not rushing, just moving like water, calmly and inevitably. One thing at a time. I can do that. Now, I'll just make myself a cup of tea....

27 March 2012

Another absolutely stunning day. Sunny, bright and warm. The weather is conspiring, for once, to get us through.

Rich and I had a horrendous time this morning, trying to get our deliveries ready for the courier to pick up. My computer didn't want to print out the FedEx labels properly, so I spent the whole day yesterday grinding my teeth and speaking to the IT guy at FedEx, trying to make it all work.

In the process, I downloaded three different browsers and two versions of Adobe Acrobat, and now my computer has gone into a sulk and completely refuses to have anything to do with the printer. Grrrr.

I'd got up at six to start the milking and found Joli, bless her, already downstairs making up the kid bottles. We both stumbled out to the barn, sleepy but glad to be alive, and enjoyed the fresh morning, the silvery crescent moon and the pink and purple sunrise. Joli then changed into her school uniform and went off to school; I turned the goats out into the already sunny field, drove Benji to school and came back to join battle with the computer.

The clock was ticking, as the FedEx order had to be filed by 10:30 a.m., and it was 10:08 when I discovered the computer simply *wasn't* going to print. It was all too much, and I burst into tears. There are a lot of things I can conquer with sheer hard work and a refusal to give up, but technology failure isn't one of them.

Rich had staggered downstairs, still looking green and haggard but not in as much pain as the day before. He held me gently while I cried myself out, and then we went back to work, finally sorting it out when I e-mailed the label to his computer, and he printed it out.

Made up the boxes, slid the labels into the official FedEx plastic slips and taped them shut. They sat there on the table, looking all official, and I was as proud of them as of the children on their first day at school. Two boxes, ready for courier pickup – but representing such a lot of hard work and such a long, long road that we've come, to reach the point where we actually have a product to sell, customers to buy it, orders, a website and a way to ship things out.

Rich and I retreated to the lounge and curled up on the sofa together for a break, and decided that we needed a new computer. Can't afford a fancy one, but we absolutely must have one that works, and a bookkeeping software package too.

Back to the office for more ordering, bottles and stickers, tape dispensers and packaging: all the things you never think you'll need until you suddenly do! Rich has gone off to get three big dumpy bags of goat food, which should see us through the time when he can't get up after the operation. They say it's a three-month recovery period. How he'll cope with that – or how I will – I hate to think.

I'm busily packing up the boxes for tomorrow's shipment of soap – our first big trade order – and I'm horribly nervous about it for some reason. I'm terrified that when it's actually time to ship, I won't have the right quantity, or something.

I've made Rich soup and probiotic and fresh ginger tea – stocking the top shelf of the fridge for him with mugs he can pop into the microwave – and instructed him firmly that he's not to eat anything else. He scared me to death yesterday after he ate the seeded wholemeal bread and was in such terrible pain. No more! If he has to live on cawl until he goes into hospital, so be it. It's my job to deliver him there in shape for his operation, and it's not going to be easy.

Would so love a nap, but maybe a big pot of coffee instead?

Later... Ridiculously, I'm suddenly feeling happy and optimistic. Have just gotten through loads of red tape for the business. There's nothing I can do about Rich's illness, but to sink my teeth into a really satisfying tangle of red tape, and emerge triumphant – well that I *can* do. It gives me an illusion of victory – and distraction.

30 March 2012

In some strange way, all this extra work seems to suit me. Like one of those cars that only really hugs the road at 80 miles an hour, I'm waking up at 6 a.m., before the alarm, coming downstairs for tea and to exercise before I go outside to milk. I never used to get up before 8 a.m. – and I wasn't consistent about stretching and warming up my back either, although I knew I should have been.

I make myself a travel cup and a Thermos of tea, and head outside. I cross the yard to the barn, pull the blue-painted door, latch it open. Inside, the goats, lying contentedly on the clean straw (or not-so-clean – note to self, remember to lay down fresh straw today), stir and bleat and struggle to their feet to put their heads over the edge of the pen, hoping to be first to be milked.

I switch on the radio and the water heater, put one bucket by the hot water tap and one by the cold, hitch up the stainless-steel milking bucket to the cutters and pipe, and scoop out a bowl of food for the first milker. I let out whoever insists on being first – usually Marmite, who's aggressive and knocks everyone else out of the way – milk the first two squirts into a plastic jug (to get rid of any possible bacteria), wipe down her teats with a disinfectant wipe, put the cluster on her, sit down to watch and take my first deep, satisfying gulp of hot sweet tea.

Yesterday the morning was so beautiful that I was literally shocked. I kept coming out of the barn and hanging over the side of the fence, trying to absorb it. The mist was hovering in the valley, and the rising sun was pouring through it, so that everything glowed, luminous and boiling, as if someone had lit it from inside. The distant sea, the bowl-shaped depression between the hills, the rust-coloured trees with their tips just turning acid green with spring – all layered over with golden, glowing steam.

I wouldn't have been surprised to see Merlin the Enchanter striding down the hill. The wizard of Arthurian legend is meant to have been born an hour from where we live – Carmarthen, or Caer Myrddin. Merlin's oak used to stand in the middle of where a roundabout is now. They even built a statue to it – an oddly modern, asymmetric abstraction of an oak.

Tiny white farmhouses all the way across the valley are the only settlements I could see. And the whole landscape was as deeply familiar and beloved as the face of a family member. I stood and breathed it in, feeling lucky for a moment.

But the stress is definitely beginning to tell. Cracks are appearing for all of us. Yesterday the goats escaped out of our woods and into a neighbour's field. I was on the phone, talking to someone about the goat show we're trying to organize, when Taid came in, shouting that the goats were out.

Rich came in and tried to get my attention, but I'd been working on getting this person on the phone for days, and so I waved my hand over my shoulder, telling Rich to wait until I was finished. He went storming off on his own, and I heard the quad bike starting. I finished the call a few minutes later and went pounding after him, but it was too late – he was gone.

I stomped all the way down the huge, long hill, through the woodlands and over the barbed-wire fence, muttering to myself. By the time I saw him, across the field, leading the runaway goats back to our fields, I was in a spitting rage, full of fear that he'd pushed himself too hard, desperately ill as he is.

'You should have waited for me!' I shouted at him ridiculously, from all the way across the field. I could barely see him, and I'm sure he couldn't hear me properly. 'Two minutes! That's all it would have taken!'

When I got closer, I pointed my finger at his face and screamed, 'Next time you wait for me!'

'All right, keep your hair on,' he said, looking confused. We shoved and pushed the goats back through the hole in the fence, cursing them and ourselves, and ruing the day we'd ever decided to keep goats.

'We could eat them,' I suggested, as we tried to corner a runaway. 'We could dine on roast goat every night for an entire month, and then we'd never have to look after them again.'

'Goat roast,' we intoned, tackling and dragging the last few bucking, kicking rebels through the mud. I'd split my welly on the barbed wire. Damn.

'Goat sausage. Goat burgers. Goat meatballs.'

But the goats just looked at us out of their long-pupilled eyes. They knew we didn't mean it.

Then yesterday Rich smashed the phone to bits during a stressful episode in which we discovered that, despite the surgeon having recommended Rich for emergency surgery, telling him to 'just turn up on the day', no-one at the hospital front desk had ever heard of Rich or knew anything about him or his paperwork.

'Pull it together!' I'd shouted at him.

'This *is* me pulled together!' he shouted back and stormed upstairs.

I looked at the smashed bits of phone handset for a minute, then picked up the other line and started again. I finally managed to reach someone who had heard of Rich – a nurse who'd talked to him in the hospital – and she promised to help sort out the paperwork.

I went upstairs and found Rich lying on the bed, looking out of the window. His skin was a horrifying shade of pale grey.

'Everything is falling apart,' he said.

'It's not,' I said stoutly. 'Everything's under control. We're doing it. We filled all our orders. It's going to be okay.'

'You don't know that,' he said.

'I do,' I said, kissing him, wishing it was true. 'I promise.'

2 April 2012

Spent the sunny Sunday yesterday making three large batches of soap – 180 bars altogether. When we start the business up again, I want to have soap ready to sell. Somehow it seems unbelievable that we'll ever be on the other side of the surgery – that Rich will be home again. I wonder how bad it will be? How different? How unbearable? From this point, there's no way of knowing.

6 April 2012

I'm sitting in the hospital, waiting for Rich to come out of surgery. He tried to tell me that there was no reason for me to be here during the operation, but I wanted to be as close to him physically as I could manage. At this moment that means the hospital café. I have an orange juice and a nice corner with my computer and our bills – at least I can get some work done while I wait!

By the time I arrived this morning, the nurses told me that Rich had already been wheeled off to the operating theatre. I didn't even get to say goodbye, or sit with him while he waited, or kiss him. I suppose the good thing is that it happened so quickly; he wouldn't have had time to worry too much or get too hungry, as they hadn't allowed him any food after midnight.

Yesterday we finished all of our preparations – a list of phone numbers and a schedule of chores, with names pencilled in next to each chore. The goat kids and orphan lambs have been farmed out to volunteers who are willing to take on the intensive job of feeding them, and friends are coming in rotation to help Joli milk on the night shift. I plan to do the morning milking daily, and then drive the two hours or so to spend the day with Rich in the hospital. Rich insisted I didn't have to be with him every day, but there's nowhere I'd rather be.

Benji is off with his bio-dad, and all the loose ends have been tied up. Stockists stocked with milk; last soap orders shipped off; 'annual leave' sign hung in the window. I want all the decks to be clear so that I can concentrate all of my attention on Rich.

Last night, after I reluctantly left the hospital, I felt tired but oddly hopeful – praying that at the end of this tunnel will be a future for us in which Rich is strong and healthy and free of pain again. When I got home Joli and Ceris were clearing the table. They had eaten a proper dinner, complete with music and candles.

Ceris had made a beautiful chicken stew while Joli milked, with the help of our good neighbour and friend Lynn – the mother of Ceris's boyfriend George. There was some of the stew left over, and I ate it hungrily, enjoying the candles that were still lit. I was so proud of the girls, carrying on as usual – and of our preparations.

I thought that it would be important for everyone to try to hit the mark of the family dinner – bang on 7:30 p.m., as usual, with fresh bread, candles and music. So there would be some structure and regularity to these crisis days. And so it seems there is. We are supported by these routines that we put into place.

I've been thinking a lot about the concept of load-bearing lately. Something that's load-bearing will hold up when you lean on it. A load-bearing wall in a house is one that you cannot remove without compromising the integrity of the structure. And some *people* are load-bearing, too, while others are not.

The kids, our routines and our neighbours are load-bearing. I've discovered through my experience of crises – when I found myself alone in a strange country with two children and no job, and now, as I'm running a farm and a new business single-handed and my husband's in hospital having a major operation – that they tend to sort your friends into two piles: load-bearing and non-load-bearing. And it's almost always a surprise, which is which.

Some people whom I would have sworn would be supportive vanished, slipping sideways and disappearing like puffballs in the wind. And some people whom I never suspected or even counted as particularly close friends, emerged rock-like from the chaos of the shifting tides. Funny how that works.

Anyhow, here I sit waiting for Rich to emerge from surgery; I'm waiting to hear our future; waiting to hear how fully he'll recover; waiting to hear, I suppose, whether he's even survived the surgery. It's a major operation, and you never know about these things.

But when I close my eyes, I see him strong, healthy and powerful again, laughing, with a huge new scar across his healed stomach. He's a fighter, my Rich. I'll have to put my faith in that – hold on to it.

Later... The nurse called me on my mobile to tell me that Rich was out of surgery, and that I could go and see him in the recovery room. I headed there as fast as I could walk, feeling absurdly nervous. When I finally found it, I rang the bell and was let in.

Rich was lying on a bed in the middle of a mostly empty room, with monitors around him and drips feeding into his arms. He looked groggy and tired but still my own, amazingly wonderful, Rich. I just sat near him and listened as he talked about how lovely the staff had been, how kind the anaesthetist was – how the man had smiled when he didn't have to.

The anaesthetist in question came by at that moment – a man with a cheerful face and a brilliantly white grin. Rich shook him by the hand and thanked him for going above and beyond the line of duty.

I was amazed by Rich, as I always am – so groggy with morphine and drugs that he could barely speak, but his impulse was of gratitude. Maybe at moments like these our core is revealed, stripped of all the coverings that we usually put over ourselves. And Rich is solid gold, right down to the core.

They moved him, after an hour or so, into the main ward. There were six beds in the room, the others occupied by men all over the age of 70, pale-skinned and ill-looking, attached to monitors and drip stands. I curled up beside Rich's bed in an armchair, my back to the rest of the ward to create an illusion of privacy.

We were both oddly high – Rich with the assortment of drugs that they'd given him, me with the relief of him having come through the surgery safely. He talked a lot, telling the same stories over and over, repeating how brilliant the anaesthetist had been. I finally left about four hours later, driving home to spread the news on the phone that he was fine, that the operation had gone well.

Later that night the surgeon stopped by to tell Rich that indeed the operation had been a success. They hadn't found anything terrible, and they expected him to make a full recovery within about six months. Victory. The result we'd been hoping for. I went to sleep feeling happy and light-hearted.

7 April 2012

Today was a different story. I thought that it might be – like running a marathon, the day after is the one to watch out for. Rich was tired, groggy, beginning to feel the pain as the huge dose of drugs for the surgery itself began to wear off after 24 hours.

He hadn't slept well in the ward, as I knew he wouldn't – he hates to be away from the farm and his own bed, doesn't travel well, can't adjust to noise and unfamiliar lights. And the other people! Like some sort of surreal painting of the rings of hell. Naked and suffering, with swollen abdomens and drip stands.

One old man across from Rich was angrily insane, telling the nurses that they were stupid, that I was weird, that he didn't belong there, and then resolutely exposing himself to the whole ward while the nurse futilely tried to get him to cover up.

Another poor soul suffered in the far corner, the only sign that he wasn't already dead the horrible wheezing and rattling of his lungs. Something terrible was happening to him, and because of the lack of privacy, we heard everything – the nurse explaining loudly that they had to operate on him right away, or he'd die; that they'd tried to contact his next of kin, but they couldn't reach her on the phone. That he'd have to sign his mark next to the cross, to consent to the operation. It was horrifying but also banal, so sort of everyday....

This, then, is the ward where no-one wants to be. Where the patients wear their insides on the outside. Where the workings of the human body are laid completely, unforgivingly bare.

And yet, I thought, at the end of the day, it was no worse than what happens on the farm. We are, after all, animals, and our functions are the same. We eat, and the food is processed and exits the bowels. Those processes continue, whether inside or outside. We're horrified by slime, by blood, by faecal matter, by afterbirth, by urine. But I've been covered with all those things in the course of working on the farm, and I know they all wash off in the washing machine.

Nothing human, by now, is alien to me. Nothing animal, either. It's all part of what we're doing here. Not so scary, when your hands are pried from your eyes, and you're forced to take a long, daylight look.

10 April 2012

Yesterday was day three after the surgery, and Rich was in a lot of pain. It's to be expected, after such a huge operation, but still difficult to watch. I get up in the morning and milk, then do some ordering on the computer (the toaster blew up; I need supplies for soap making when we start the business up again...) and then leave the house around noon, to arrive at the hospital around 2 p.m.

I stay until 6:30 p.m., reading bits of the newspaper out loud, chatting idly, just being in the room with Rich. I drive home, arriving after 8 p.m. The girls are cleaning up the remains of supper by then. Joli and I watch some TV, and then I fall into bed. Amazing that this pattern already feels like a routine.

Rich has been moved into his own private room, through some kind of miracle that I don't understand but for which I'm deeply grateful. I seem to be more excited about it than he is. He said yesterday that he might as well have been out in the hallway, for all the difference it made to how he felt. But for me, the solace of the small room with its door that closes, away from the sounds and smells of the other occupants of the outside ward, is the next thing to heaven.

I've started bringing in lemongrass essential oil, from the soap making, and dabbing it on pieces of kitchen roll and leaving it around the room. It makes a heavenly scent. The nurses love it, and use every excuse to come into this room and take a deep breath – it does lift the spirit.

Suddenly, Rich opened his eyes and said, 'I forgot to get rid of the lambs.' Two of them had died, along with one of the sheep. We'd called the knacker man to take away the sheep.

'Why didn't you just have him take the lambs as well?' I asked.

'I was going to do it myself, but I just forgot,' he replied.

'And they've been sitting there ever since?'

'I guess so.'

A wave of rage swept through me. Stupid, stupid, stupid and careless. How ridiculous, not to just have them all taken away at once. And now I was going to have to deal with it. Not on day one of the death, either, but nearly a week later, when the corpses would have turned into the stuff of nightmares. It was too much. Just too much.

'Just take them and drop them into the pit,' Rich said. I stared back at him.

'I'm not going to do that,' I said. 'I'm just not.' I imagined getting the corpses into the wheelbarrow, fighting to get it down the long, slippery, muddy hill, manoeuvring the lid off the tank pit with a shovel, dropping the bodies in. No – too much. 'I'll call the knacker man,' I said.

'Get Rhys to do it.' Rich suggested. Rhys – Rich's brother – has offered to help, and means it.

'I'm not asking Rhys to do that.'

'Then I'll phone him and ask him myself.'

'I don't think you should.' It's too much to ask. Rhys is endlessly kind and helpful but he's not a farmer, hardened to these things in the way Rich is. He's a gardener, and a physics professor. He would most likely be as horrified by the task as I was.

'I will sort it,' I tell him firmly, and I will. Somehow. Because I have to. It has to be done, and there's no-one else to do it. We change the subject. I want to scream at him, but I can't, of course. He can't help having forgotten, and it's too late to fix it.

But later, sitting in the car waiting to summon my energy for the long drive home, I grip the edge of the steering wheel and weep. Not for Rich, but because I'm furious at him. How dare he put me in this situation? It's just the one thing too much.

I got home and put off dealing with the dead lambs – I was too tired, and surely I didn't need to do it after a long stint at the hospital? I dreamed about those damn lambs all night, and got up dreading it. I'd milk first, I decided, and then go and look – see how big they were, and how horrible, and whether or not I could manage to get them down into the disposal pit.

11 April 2012

Joli had a lie-in this morning. I'd allowed her to stay up late last night, as a special treat – she'd been working like a grown woman and it seemed unfair to make her go to bed early, like a child. Luckily for me, she's on spring break at the moment. We'd sat up together and watched multiple episodes of *Friends*, from the much-loved DVD set I'd given her for Christmas.

But by 10 a.m. I found myself getting increasingly annoyed as the time passed, and she didn't appear. Finally she showed up, and I told her brusquely that she needed to be up by 9 a.m. in future. She nodded apologetically and set off on her round of chores.

The lambs sat uncomfortably at the edge of my consciousness all the while I was finishing the milking, and when I couldn't find anything else to do, I sighed and headed up towards the top barn.

I met Joli coming down. 'I've sorted the lambs,' she said, matter-of-factly.

I goggled at her. 'What do you mean, you've sorted them?'

'I dragged them out and put them where the knacker man can reach them.'

'You did?' I couldn't seem to make my brain work.

'Yes,' she replied, looking at me strangely.

'Was it – was it horrible?' I asked.

'Not too bad,' she said. 'Only they were stiff. I don't mind dead things – it's just the stiffness that freaks me out.'

'Would you like... would you like me to book you a facial?' I said.

'Yes, please!' she said happily, and linked her arm in mine as we walked inside. I picked up the phone and booked her a facial straight away. My girl.

12 April 2012

Rich is coming home today! I feel excited and strangely shocked, and a little afraid. How will we cope? Might something happen to him medically that I won't know how to deal with? It's been difficult but strangely peaceful, this little time when my only duties have been to milk in the morning and then make the long trek to the hospital.

But now I imagine the immediate future coming towards me like a huge wall of water – Rich home, impatient and in pain; the business starting up again; people knocking on the door, wanting things, wanting to buy milk; Benji at home, and both kids needing to be taken to school.

It's been a hard-won island of quiet, this period while Rich has been in hospital. I schemed and organized and called in all my favours, wearing out the goodwill of our friends and neighbours.

But now it's about to end. And what then? Who'll help me when Rich is home on the couch needing tending, the two big girls are both back at university and Joli is busy with homework? How will I manage it all?

13 April 2012

Rich has been home for one full day and so far, it's not too difficult to manage. The toilet isn't working, though – another problem – and normally Rich handles all the plumbing. I suggested calling a plumber, which he wouldn't hear of. But how do we solve it, if he's not strong enough to do it himself, and won't let me call someone else to fix it? This, too, is out of my range.

The evening milking needs to start at 5:30 p.m. If it doesn't, we end up not eating supper until 9 p.m, too late for Benji and too late for me, these days. Yesterday, we defrosted some pea soup that I'd cooked and frozen in the weeks before Rich went into hospital. But since Elly, Ceris and George were all going to be home, bringing our tally around the dinner table up to eight, I could see that it wasn't going to be enough food, even with the loaf of bread I had in the oven.

I needed to go to the store to get more ham to put in the soup, more sour cream to add to a new batch of soup, but I was out of cash to hand to one of the girls, so they couldn't go for me. If I went to the store myself, the milking wouldn't start until 6:30 p.m. and dinner would be unspeakably late.

Joli was in the nearby town of Carmarthen – I'd sent her to go have fun with her friends, after she'd done all the morning chores for me. I was so exhausted that I fell back into bed and slept straight through until 2 p.m. I was shivery and shaky and dreaded falling ill – I mustn't, at this point; I can't.

Luckily I slept off the ill feeling and got up with enough energy to make a batch of soap. I can feel the tide of the re-opening business headed towards us on Monday (today is Friday), with very little soap in stock.

But the immediate problem – more groceries, to feed more people. I stomped out the door in a rage and got into the girls' new (used) little blue car. (I'd loaned mine to Elly, so that she could go pick up Joli in Carmarthen.)

I stormed up the driveway and had a shock when I tried to set the handbrake for the steep hill start at the top of the drive, and nothing happened. I just slid merrily backwards – the handbrake had no effect at all. By the time I managed to rev the engine enough to get it going against gravity, I was halfway back down the drive. I eventually managed to do the shopping – thankfully the shop is only two minutes away – and came back with the fresh supplies.

I reported that the car wasn't roadworthy and that it would have to be fixed before it was driven again; Ceris had been planning to drive it to work the next day. Luckily her boyfriend George came in at that very moment (he's a mechanic) and I asked him if he would get the parts and fix it before he leaves on his year-long trip to Australia.

Ceris is being very stoical about him going, at least on the outside, but it must be tearing her up on the inside. They're both so young, it's hard to imagine that their relationship will survive an entire year apart. But then again, so far they've surprised me at every turn! They got together at age 17, and have been as monogamous as swans ever since. George lives in the farmhouse with us – he and Ceris have a large room at the back of the house – and he's completely a member of the family.

Such a lovely young man. What we'll do without him, I cannot imagine. He drives Joli to the school bus every morning at 7.45 a.m. – another chore that'll fall back on my shoulders after he goes.

George said that he'd fix the car but that it would take him a week to get the parts and do the repairs. Ceris will have to use my car until that time. I have to go and pick up the lambs from Debbie, who's been feeding them while Rich was in hospital. But I suppose I can use Rich's Land Rover for that, since he's not using it. How complicated does life really *need* to be?

15 April 2012

I cried a lot on Friday. I cried when we found out that the toilet was really broken. I cried again when it turned out that it wasn't just broken but the cistern was cracked, and it needed to be replaced. I cried again when it looked like the freezer had packed in, and all of our buckets of frozen milk were slowly thawing.

It felt like the universe had turned upside down, and was dumping itself on my head....

Luckily all of it resolved, with some help from a wonderful family. *Perthyn* to the rescue! Rhys went out the very next morning, bought a new toilet for us, and spent the whole of the early afternoon installing it. I moved a bunch of frozen milk into the freezer that I thought was broken, and brought the temperature back down. So even if it's broken, it's maintaining – for the moment. A bit like me...

16 April 2012

Well, it's 11 days post-op and Rich is well on the mend, thank goodness. He was better all round yesterday – feeling better, mood seemed better, more energy. He's lost a lot of weight and looks a bit gaunt, but his colour is improving. Not that horrible grey-green colour that he used to turn.

I'm struggling to know what to feed him now. I want to give him food that'll support his recovery, but the things that I think of as 'healthy' don't seem to be on the menu – he's not supposed to have oatmeal, whole grains, brown bread, oranges or fruit with skin.

I usually buy a book and research when I find myself in this situation, but this one seems harder to crack – plus I don't usually cook lunch. We have tea and toast in the morning before milking, then come in for a big egg and bacon protein breakfast around 11 a.m. We have a snack around 3 or 4 p.m. and then I put a big farm supper on the table around 8 p.m.

So I'm not accustomed to having to serve up lunch, and I think Rich is feeling a bit neglected during the day – I'm spinning so fast, trying to keep the whole farm running, that I don't have time to sit with him, the way I did in the hospital.

Business starts again today – here we go!

19 April 2012

Tuesday night was a real low point. I'd hit the ground running at 6 a.m., and run all day until past 10 at night. I was desperately looking forward to sitting down on the couch to watch half an hour of TV, but I couldn't even do that, because I had to go out to the barn to feed the goat kids before I went to sleep. I stomped out, fed them, stomped back in. My recreation time was gone, and I knew that I'd have to drop straight into bed if I wanted any chance of making it through the next day.

Rich was in the kitchen, trying to get the lid onto the leftovers box, and it wouldn't go.

I went over to him. 'Here, let me.'

But I couldn't do it either, and as I struggled, the fragile edge of my control suddenly turned sideways and disappeared.

'Close, you f^&*^&!' I screamed, beating the box with my fist. I burst into tears.

Rich took it away from me, put it in the fridge and came back to hold me while I sobbed uncontrollably. He led me up to bed while I cried some more, and then we went to sleep.

But oddly, in the morning, I felt better. Or maybe not oddly – isn't that what they always say? Things will look better in the morning? For no better reason than that you're rested, I guess.

But it suddenly occurred to me that this really isn't so hard. I mean, for goodness sake, all I'm doing is putting milk into bottles. The goats are doing the really amazing part – producing this healing stuff out of grass. All I have to do is get it out of them and into bottles, and put labels on. Some of the milk I put goat's milk kefir grains in, let it sit and strain it out. Hardly rocket science. I can do this. I know I can. It's just not that hard.

And with that knowledge, I went out in a good mood. I drew a funny picture for Joli, and made her a cup of tea that I left on the table. And when she came out, she was in a good mood too. It changed everything, for both of us.

24 April 2012

I was on an odd high for a couple of days after that last realization. I actually started to love getting up early, getting out into the barn, doing all the milking. We had the loveliest day on the weekend – bright sun – and I went out into the swing-set yard with the goat kids. I sat on the grass, and they crowded around me, piling into my lap and standing still to be stroked.

I hadn't really cuddled them since before they went to the Grants to be fostered, and I was surprised by the intensity of their determination to be petted. It was blissful, being surrounded by baby animals and soaking up the sun.

Joli and I made batches of the new Break-Out Magic Cleanser, which has thyme and tea tree essential oils in it. The facial clay gives it a gorgeous pale green colour, like new leaves. For some reason the powerful essential oil combination makes it set very quickly, so we struggled to get it out of the pan and into the moulds in time. But the resulting facial bars smell delicious, and work a treat... Joli swears by them, and her teenage skin is looking lovely!

All was satisfying and contented in the kitchen as I stirred the soap and Joli packed and wrapped the cut bars. The radio was on, we chatted as our hands were busy, and the sharp scents of thyme and tea tree floated on the air.

On the Sunday, we bottled kefir, as we'd had a big order come in. We stood around the table. I filtered the kefir; Joli poured, and Rich labelled the bottles. I love looking at the ranks of small white bottles when we're finished, all neatly capped and standing like little soldiers. I never thought I'd enjoy 'manufacturing' things so much.

But it's fantastic, to make something that didn't exist before, out of things from your own patch of land. Even better if people want these things, and are willing to buy them. And if you can make a living from it – well, that's as good as it gets.

We'll have to see about the making-a-living part. Rich is out of work at the moment, after his operation, and has been denied any disability benefits. My father gave us a hugely generous sum of money as an early birthday present, and we've been trickling along on that. But soon enough that tide will diminish, and we'll scrape the rocky bottom again. Will our little bottles be enough to keep us afloat?

On Sunday night, I was milking when Joli came flying into the barn. I knew by the look on her face that something was terribly wrong, and my heart seized in my chest.

'Taid's fallen,' she said. I left the goat on the milking stand and ran after her as quickly as I could in my wellies.

Taid, my 76-year-old, pipe-smoking, fiercely independent father-in-law emerges every morning around 11 a.m., with hat and scarf wrapped rather dashingly round his throat to drive up to Aberaeron to pick up a prescription, or go up to the supermarket for a newspaper and tobacco for his beloved pipe. (A diagnosis of emphysema has not dimmed this love – he still smokes away, and we've reluctantly agreed that, at his age, he has a right to do as he pleases.)

He still takes care of his chickens – moved, at my insistence, away from the steep, muddy and slippery hill where I feared he'd fall and break a hip – into a more contained chicken house where they don't have to be let out and shut in every night, and can be fed only every three days.

I don't check on him as a matter of course – he's proud and doesn't like it. He comes out when he wants to: for a visit or a cup of coffee, or just to see what's happening on the farm. He eats a hot meal with us in the evening, and then retreats back into his tobacco-smoky den, to read and watch TV.

He's had a difficult time lately – on top of the two big heart attacks and two major strokes that he survived before I came to live at the farm. He's recently had prostate surgery, a bronchial infection that nearly landed him back in hospital, and a mini stroke that left him wandering, blindly, into our kitchen, having temporarily lost the ability to see.

He recovered from all of these episodes, and seemed as strong as ever. But now as I raced into the house, I ran the possibilities through my mind, and none of them was good. The reality was worse than I'd feared. He lay on the floor, face down, half twisted to the side. I ran over to him and dropped to my knees. Rich was on the phone, trying to get through to the ambulance service. I looked at Taid's twisted form – his breathing was harsh, laboured, wrong. Had he broken anything when he fell? I didn't want to move him, just in case. But it seemed horrible to leave him as he was.

I couldn't think of anything to do for him. So I started to pray – it was all I had. I prayed for peace for all of us, and strength. I prayed for healing, and for the pain to depart, and for a vast river of golden light to come down and enfold Taid, carrying away all his hurts and troubles. He liked that – he seemed calmer.

Rich came through and said the ambulance men had told him they were on their way and that we should get Taid onto his back so he could breathe better, never mind about possible injuries. I started to try to turn him over and found to my horror that he was too heavy to move on my own – Joli was going to have to help me. Rich couldn't help, as it was still too soon after his surgery.

I called Joli, and she came, and together we pushed and hauled until we got Taid onto his back. But his limbs were still distorted and in a strangely wrong position. I looked at him, trying to work out how to make him more comfortable. At least we could get his dressing gown off – the room was boiling hot and stuffy, from the electric heater. We worked off his dressing gown. I should check the damage, I thought.

He was conscious, that much I knew. He could hear and respond. I asked him to move each part. Everything worked on the right – nothing on the left. I asked him to use his right hand, which was strong, to give me one finger for yes and two for no. We worked out through this system that he was uncomfortable, and then through an odd series of '20 questions' that he wanted to sit up.

I looked around – he was too far from a couch or chair, and too heavy to move. So I would have to be his chair. I got behind him on the floor and propped him up in my arms, to ease his breathing. Joli brought some pillows, and I put them behind his head, kneeling behind him with my arms around him.

'I'm so sorry, Taid,' I said, tears filling my eyes, and kissed the top of his head, which was just in front of my chin. 'I'm so sorry.' I knelt behind him like that for a long time, holding him up so that he could breathe until the ambulance men came in their green uniforms; until someone told me gently that he would take over. And then they took him to hospital.

27 April 2012

The massive stroke that swept through Taid's body took the entire left side. And now he has pneumonia. There seems little doubt that he's dying. And we're waiting, in a horrible limbo.

Rhys went in the ambulance with him on Sunday night. I went to sit in with Taid on Monday, and again on Tuesday. Yesterday I didn't go – Rich seemed very low, and I didn't want to leave him alone. It frightens me, how tired he is, how pale. He was just starting to get better, when this happened, and it seems to have knocked him right back again. Rich has been forbidden to go into the hospital because of the risk of infection to his still fresh wound. So he can't see his dying father. It's very hard. But we can't run the risk.

1 May 2012

I'm not normally a religious person – don't go to church. But at the moment, my God is the sun over the sea, and the familiar, beloved contours of the land as it curves over the valley. My own private vision each night as I come out of the barn. Last night, gold and magenta and peach, like hot wax spilled over a silver-bright ocean....

Still waiting. Taid took another turn for the worse last night. In a strange way, it was almost a relief – they've been aggressively treating the pneumonia that would have carried him off in the first few days, but there's no response from him. No awareness, no consciousness, no hand squeezing as there was in the beginning.

It occurred to me how cruel it is that modern medicine has so cleverly strengthened the bars of the cage – 100 years ago, nature would have taken its course, and after the stroke he would have peacefully drifted off. Now they've cured his body just enough that he can't escape it – and he remains trapped.

When I visited Taid, I took a CD player from his house and some of the CDs that he loved. Loretta Lynn, Slim Williams, Patsy Cline. I took lavender essential oil from my soap making, and a Bible to read out loud. I put the lavender around the room, so that the air smelled sweet, and turned on the music, and began to read. The beautiful words of the Psalms, triumphant and victorious, comforted me at least, if Taid couldn't hear them.

I drove the girls to the hospital last night. What they saw was frightening – Taid's mouth open, breathing harsh, oxygen mask, tubes coming out, sensors beeping. Nothing like the way we remember him properly, the way he really was – a feisty, proud old man with his white beard and hat and scarf, striding out to feed the chickens, blue eyes striking sparks.

4 May 2012

Taid died two days ago. The grief is almost easier to bear than thinking of him trapped and suffering.

I put pictures of him on the windowsill, with a little vase of flowers and a candle, and we all piled onto the sofa in a big family sandwich; we watched the candle flicker, and said whatever came into our heads to say.

At suppertime, I moved one of the pictures – the one I love best of him, wearing an orange life jacket, arms flung out like Zorba the Greek – to his empty seat and put candles either side. We broke open a bottle of champagne, put on some of Taid's favourite music and toasted him. Everyone said something as we went around the table, and everyone lifted their glass and drank – even Benji. The funeral is at the end of this week.

A bad day today – I've been feeling tired and weepy and miserable. Rich's blood test showed a raised inflammatory level, which could be due to some kind of infection or stress. Well, there's certainly been plenty of that around!

He's four weeks into his recovery, still sleeping all the time and starting to stoop as the scar pulls. So cruel, for him to have to suffer through all this grief and trouble, just as he's trying to heal. So cruelly unfair, all of it.

Rhys is sorting out all the death details and paperwork – fair play to him. The funeral director came around to the house the other day to discuss the funeral, and Rich and Rhys, and their sister Cath, sat in with him. I didn't have to do any of that organizing, thankfully, as I'm not sure I could take on one more thing at the moment. I'm not working on the soap or the cream the way that I'd like to at the moment, as I'm occupied with the milk and the kefir.

I'm getting up now at 5 a.m. and working straight through the day until 10:20 p.m., when I fall into bed exhausted and sleep deeply, dreamlessly, unless Benji wakes me up crying in the night. Joli offered to milk for me the other night and I refused, almost panicked – I just milk, I must milk; milking is what I do, morning and night; it's what I have to hold on to. I worked so hard to get to the point where I can do it all on my own, I'm almost afraid to stop now. Afraid that if I do, it'll break me.

10 May 2012

I've taken to reading my beloved farm landscape like a set of personal runes, scanning it for meaning and significance each morning as I head towards the barn, and home again in the evening. On a particularly dismal day, the sky was silver-grey, the sun a flat disc nearly obscured, only a faintly brighter silver.

I smiled in recognition – cloudy, but still present. Just. A perfect description for my own state. Another day, brighter, gave me bands of blue sky over the sea – increasing clarity. I can't tell whether my state comes first and affects the clouds, or the clouds affect my state, but they always seem to match, perfectly.

Today is the day of Taid's funeral. I'm dreading it, mostly because of Rich. It's such a long day – the car comes to pick us up at 11 a.m., we drive to the chapel, have the service there, then the long drive to the crematorium, service there, then the drive to the hotel where the buffet will be held, then the drive home.

I dread the thought of Rich standing in the rain, being pushed past his endurance by all the well-intentioned people trying to comfort him – who siphon off the last of his energy, without realizing or meaning to....

Yesterday he had an appointment with Dr Mark Thomas, our brilliant local GP. Dr Mark is so popular that it's nearly impossible to get to see him, but worth it when you do. One month after surgery, Rich just hasn't been feeling right. He's still so incredibly exhausted, and has a strange pain when he lies down at night, although the pain doesn't seem to trouble him during the day. He's dizzy when he stands up – it seems that he has low blood pressure.

I went in with him – I always do go to his appointments, if I possibly can – and was expecting to hear Dr Mark make reassuring noises about the amount of time that recovering from surgery takes.

But he wasn't reassuring – not at all. In fact, he took Rich's blood pressure, and it was so low that he took it twice more, just to be sure. Then he ordered an emergency blood test and started mentioning the possibility of Addison's disease. Very rare, he said. He's only seen it once in 25 years, but just to be sure....

My stomach clenched as he listed the possible causes – a rapid withdrawal from steroids, an operation or insult to the body, an auto-immune issue... Rich has had them all. The doctor phoned to make sure that the blood test could be processed right away, then looked at us levelly. 'The office is closing for training this afternoon,' he said. 'But if the result of this blood test is positive, I'll give it to the after-hours doctor. He'll contact you, and you'll need to go straight to the hospital.'

My ears started to ring, and I could hardly hear what he was saying. A home blood-pressure monitor – yes, we could buy one, right away. He wanted to know the results of our on-going monitoring tomorrow. 'We can't,' Rich said. 'Tomorrow is my father's funeral.'

I cut him off. 'Of course we can,' I said firmly. 'I'll phone from the car as we follow the hearse.'

I went off to buy a blood-pressure monitor and put in the new prescription for Rich's pain medication, while he went to have his bloods taken. Hope against hope, he may be suffering a bad reaction from the previous pain pills, and that's all it is. Please, please. I locked myself in the car and cried hard for about two minutes, then wiped my eyes, took a deep breath, and drove to the pharmacy. This couldn't happen. It couldn't. Not after everything we've been through. Please.

We didn't tell any of the kids what had happened when we got home, only that Rich had low blood pressure. As soon as I had a private moment, I dashed to the computer and looked up Addison's disease. I felt icy cold as I scanned the article quickly – chronic, immune system turning on the adrenal glands; life-long medication required. Surely, surely not.

I went into the living room, where Rich was installed on the sofa in front of the fire. He looked up at me – so pale, so grey, it twisted my heart. He knew right away what I'd been doing.

'You looked it up?' he said. I nodded.

'Tell me?'

I put my head on his shoulder. 'I can't,' I whispered. 'Do you want to read it? I'll bring in the laptop.'

'No,' he shook his head. 'I'd rather not know. I don't have it, anyway.'

'You'd better not,' I said.

We waited all day for the phone call, and finally, at 5 p.m., my control broke and I phoned the after-hours doctor. He'd never heard of Rich, and no results had come through. A good sign, surely? Or just bureaucratic incompetence? I'll phone first thing in the morning. Please, please...

The next day was like some kind of bad play. Old friends – well-wishers – showed up with flowers for Taid, while I was still on the phone to the out-of-hours doctor, and of course my call was so important that I couldn't hang up immediately.

Then the funeral director arrived and was led into the room, as well. It was so full there was almost no place for him to sit. Then Elly phoned Ceris to ask for a lift home from Swansea University, where she's studying psychology, and Ceris, who'd agreed to keep an eye on the supper, came to tell me that she was going to have to set out on the two-hour drive to get Elly. She passed me the timer that would beep when the bread rolls were ready.

Meanwhile, Joli and I had to go out to milk – the goats must be milked morning and night, tragedies or emergencies notwithstanding. It was getting later and later, and we know by now that going out to milk after 6 p.m. means we won't be eating until 8.

I took the bread timer into the room full of company, waved at everyone, apologized, and asked Rich to keep an eye on the bread. Then I sat down, in the blessed warmth, and enjoyed a chat with our visitors for just a few minutes – such a luxury, and enough to make me very, very late, but it was irresistible.

Then we finally went out to milk. Ceris and Elly phoned in to report; they were driving cross-country, making their way back to the farm slowly, stopping off at emergency rooms and out-of-hours GP surgeries, as Elly hadn't been feeling well. The stress of Rich's illness and Taid's death has been telling on all the children as well. I feel like I can barely help them with all that's going on; goodness knows how they're coping.

I can only imagine what the girls' trip home must have been like – they were still not back when Rich and I went to bed at 10:30 p.m. Poor Ceris – she's been so stalwart lately, and struggling with her own issues as she goes through teacher training. Poor Elly. Poor all of us.

Next day Ceris asked Rich what was wrong with me, and Rich said, 'She's just hammered (exhausted).' Sweetly, Ceris offered to do the school run for me, a trip that would involve leaving at 7:45 a.m., taking Joli on a 15-minute trip to Cardigan, then swinging back to pick up Benj at 8:15 and taking him 10 minutes in the other direction.

I stared at her blankly. 'Are you sure?' I wouldn't ask anyone else to take it on – it's a lengthy car journey. I always time the morning milking so that I'm finished just in time to jump in the car.

I'm sure,' she said. She went on to pick Joli up later in the day, when Joli missed her bus home, and collected Benji from jujitsu. Bless her. Ceris has had an unbelievably hard day. Only slightly less hard than mine – because she doesn't know what I know. Or what I dread.

How Ceris and Elly will get through the funeral today, I don't know. Or Rich. Benji is being picked up by his bio-dad, so he's okay. Not going to the funeral, as we want him to remember Taid as he was, and not be frightened or upset.

Later... Just had the news from the doctor – Rich is clear! Thank God! No Addison's disease. No anything else, for that matter. Infection wise, that is. Just a bad reaction to his pain medication. I burst into tears, from sheer relief. I thought that it just couldn't be – surely we're due for a break. Thank God, thank goodness. He had all the symptoms, and all the causes, and I thought... but never mind, it's not true. I feel so happy and relieved; the rest of the day will seem like a picnic. Seems odd to say, but everything is put into perspective now. Addison's – no, unthinkable. At least one cup has passed from us. Thank you, Lord.

I only remember snippets of the funeral. Raining – umbrellas folded, shaking off raindrops, as people came into the chapel. The trip afterwards in the big black car to the crematorium. Rich beside me, blessedly solid and warm. The finality of the coffin sliding behind the velvet curtains....

13 May 2012

In the personal rune set that the farm has become for me, today everything is sunny and newly washed. The sea is the brightest blue and the sky completely clear. Exactly! I feel exactly the same.

Rich had his first really good day yesterday, five weeks after the operation. He slept well and had the energy to be up and on his feet all day. Hallelujah! We may pay for it today, but it's a sign that he's finally well and truly healing. I'm still so deeply relieved that he doesn't have Addison's disease that the mere thought can bring tears to my eyes.

Rhys and Cath came around to sort out Taid's flat. It took all day, as they sifted through clothes, books and family treasures.

I've been angry at Taid, I realize. It's a cliché of the grieving process, and so I resist it. But it's true. I've been angry at him for leaving us, for leaving an empty chair at the table, for leaving the empty flat echoing with his footsteps.

But yesterday, as I clutched my ever-present cup of tea and seized a minute during the milking to pop out of the barn and stare out over our beloved swoop of land down to the sea, watching the sun turn the water into flat beaten copper with a glaze of apricot, I was suddenly visited with a flush of release. Of gratitude, and forgiveness. It felt almost as though Taid was standing there at my shoulder. I felt love for the fierce old man, and a sincere wish that wherever he was now, he was happy and where he wanted to be.

Suddenly I saw a vision of him as he must have been in his prime – black-bearded and broad-shouldered, striding up to the college lectern in his flowing robes, looking every bit the teacher he'd been all his life. Then I had a vivid mental image of him on the beach, trousers rolled up to his knees, walking hand in hand with a slim, young Biddy – Richard's mother, the girls' grandmother – as in a photo I'd once seen. They looked so happy and so young.

And then, abruptly, it seemed as though I could feel Taid's presence at my elbow, seeking, pressing, looking out over the view with me. He used to love this view as much as I do, and we'd often stop together, he in his purple plaid coat and hat, walking stick in hand, me wrapped in layers of fleece, headed for the barn. We'd stand silently, the pair of us, looking out together over the green and russet patchwork of trees and fields, the rolling curves of the mountains opening to the sea.

I could feel him standing there with me now, and I knew what he wanted.

'I will, Taid, I'll take care of them,' I promised him. 'All the people you love. And the farm. I'll stay here, and help look after it all.'

This is my place now: the wet and rolling and green hills, the white farmhouse with its plume of smoke, the sheep with the black faces, the goat on the weather vane.

And the sea. Always, the sea.

10 July 2012

I spend a lot of time crying in the barn. For some reason, it's an incredibly soothing place to cry – there's no-one to see me there and to be upset by the fact that I'm crying, and the thumping of the milking machine in the background is steadying.

I cry sometimes from tiredness, and sometimes from feeling overwhelmed, but mostly it's about Rich. He has to go back into hospital to have yet another massive operation, and it seems so monstrously unfair as he's only just recovered from the last one. It's supposed to be on 10 September! That's only eight weeks away!

A massive abdominal operation that will entail four hours in the operating room and three months of painful recovery. And then yet another, smaller, operation afterwards. The first operation was to remove the colon. The second one will be to reconstruct what they call a 'J-pouch' in his intestine, which then has to be left to heal for a period of time. And then a third – and hopefully final – operation to remove the colostomy bag, and hook up the new plumbing.

He'll have the bag in place until the third operation. And hopefully, if all goes well, after the third operation he'll be free of the bag and back to normal – as normal as you can be, without a colon. That's if we're lucky. And it all goes to plan.

I don't have to face all that pain myself – although I would happily share it if I could, if it would make it less. But I can't. It's Rich who has to go through all of that again. And he knows, this time, exactly what he's in for.

And so do I. It'll be another three months of running the farm on my own. But this time, I'm determined to have outside help. Rich and Ceris (home from university for the summer, having just graduated from her early childhood education programme) have been painting Taid's flat, and it's going to be beautiful once it's re-floored and decorated.

My parents can stay there if we can get it ready in time for their arrival in a month's time. And after that, I'll advertise for someone who wants to come and stay on a farm for a couple of months – in their own flat with a kitchen, lounge and bedroom, and sea views from every window.

And in the meantime, there's hope. There must be hope. It's going to be a long, rocky road in front of us – but at the end of that road is Rich, strong and healthy, vigorous, free of the pain. We have to stay focused on that.

5 September 2012

Just put my mom on the plane, after a blissful month of having her here with us. We did a lot of thinking and talking... Rich is going into hospital in four days.

We talked about fear. I think maybe there are different kinds of fear. Sometimes fear can be helpful – for example, when it sharpens your instincts and keeps you out of trouble. But what do you do about *this* kind of fear – when you can't do anything to avoid it? Like a soldier going into battle. Rich will inevitably go into hospital, where they'll cut him open in a long and gruelling operation. I will inevitably have to run everything while he's gone. There's no avoiding this pain – and knowing that fact causes unavoidable fear. But since fear isn't helpful – or avoidable – is it the same as sadness?

Funny that no-one tells you about these things. I don't recall being taught what to do about pain, or the different kinds of fear, and whether they should be handled differently. I've an ominous feeling that I'm going to get to test out all my pretty theories, very soon.

I asked Rich what he was doing with his fear, and he said that he wasn't very afraid of the pain of the operation. All his fears, he said, centre around me – that I will do too much, fall apart. And of course, all my fears centre around him. Maybe that's what happens, when you love someone? I've never properly loved a man before, so it's all a bit of a revelation to me.

7 September 2012

A good day yesterday. Shockingly, it was a happy day. The sun most obligingly came out just in time for us to get the hay off the fields – Rich hired someone to come in and bale one field with the big baler, so that we can sell the bales. The second field, which is our chemical-free hay that we feed our milking goats, he's going to bale today, and everyone is coming around to help get the bales off the field tonight.

Rich was super-charged all day yesterday – I call it his 'hay high' – sunburned and energetic and working dawn to dusk. It's his adrenaline, his life, out there with the hay and the tractors, and I love to see him loving it.

I got up at 6 a.m. today and milked, as always. Our new helper, Magalie, who's staying in the guest cottage in exchange for helping out, fed the young stock and filtered and bottled the milk. It was all done and washed out by 8:30 a.m. Then Rich and I both walked Benji to school – Benji in his smart new uniform, holding our hands on either side. Rich and I walked back home together, more slowly, still holding hands. The last time that he'll be able to walk Benji to school for many, many months. The last time for so many things as we count down the days until I drive him to hospital and come home without him.

I'm thinking that life may be normal again by New Year's. I'm not looking for anything until then. From now until Christmas, we'll just snug in and let Rich recover. I'm going to get him a sheepskin for the couch, and I've ordered loads of DVDs – *Happy Days*, *Fawlty Towers* and *The Waltons*, *Bewitched* and *I Dream of Jeannie*, all the comforting shows from the 70s that I remember made me laugh. It's the only thing I can do, to prepare for the time ahead.

Sunshine coming and going, but out at the moment – we need a full day, just one full day of precious sun, for the hay to be ready this afternoon, and then we'll be prepared for the winter, like squirrels with their nuts tucked safely away.

17 September 2012

I was standing outside the barn after milking, watching the clouds moving and shifting over our mysterious landscape. Somehow, here at the farm, the bowl of the sea and the horizon actually seem to be higher up than the place where we're standing – as if here, on top of our hill, we're below sea level. As if the bowl of sea and sky could tip in over us. But it never does.

There was a slight rain, and grey clouds, but the whole landscape was lit with a mysterious light that came from nowhere that I could see – as if lit from within.

Watching the clouds moving, I thought, *That's it. That's the way that everything is.* Constantly moving, constantly shifting. And wishing otherwise is as foolish as getting attached to a cloud picture that you see while you're lying on your back, staring into the sky. Of course, it'll shift and break – of course it will. Do you cry when the dragon you see turns into a witch, and then into a pillow? No – because you expect it of clouds.

The problem that we have is the *illusion* of permanence. You think that the stone house is solid and forever, that the marriage will stand, that the family will never change. Because it looks solid in the moment – more solid than cloud – you think that it is solid.

But it isn't. Its rate of change is simply slower than the clouds. Because you can't see it shifting during your attention span – say, half an hour – you think it's unchanging.

Our attention spans are relative. A rock changes – but it takes hundreds or thousands of years to do it. A plant moves – but it moves within a 24-hour cycle, and our restless natures can't sit still long enough to watch. So we think that plants are insensate – that they can't feel, or move – because they don't do it during the time span when we're patient enough to watch. But they do. And when you set a 24-hour camera on them, you can see them do it.

So everything changes – but at different times, and at different rates. Like alternating sine waves. Just like – yes – a symphony. Like the treble and bass clef notes of music, shifting together but in different times. The basso notes of rock and mountain, planet and star, changing slowly. The mezzo soprano notes of bug and microorganism – tiny, quick, pattering lives, shifting so quickly that it's difficult to hear.

The alto of tree, tiger, monkey and human, plant and bear, all in their interwoven song. It must have been what Beethoven heard. It must have been why it didn't matter to him, being deaf. He could still hear what mattered, inside his head. He understood.

And it explains, as well, something that I've never quite grasped before – the gypsies. I've always been intrigued by them – by their mysterious nature of always journeying, never arriving. It's said that they have no idea of ownership, which is why they 'steal' things, and are therefore hated and feared by rooted communities.

I've always wondered why the gypsies' strange, atonal, dissonant way of life strikes such a chord of fascination with me, and with many others. Their delicate but complete refusal of the attachment to bricks and mortar that so defines the rest of us; their subtle assertion of the fact that it's better to be always travelling, than to arrive. I think that their way of life mimics most truly the way of things – that's why they fascinate us.

I'm so afraid of change at the moment – afraid that this fragile stability we have will be swept away, and what replaces it will be terrible. But there's no point in trying to hang on to anything. Everything changes. That's the only thing we know for sure. Our bricks and mortar give us the illusion of stability. But it's only an illusion.

The gypsies understand – or understood once, some time deep in the misty past – that stability is an illusion. They grasped the fact that pretending that anything is stable – that anything really stands still – is futile. And ultimately only causes pain.

Is it better then, to define your entire life so that there's no illusion of stability? Nothing to hang on to, nothing that allows you to pretend? That's how reality is, so why not embrace it, all at once? Build ye empires and houses all you like. They crumble in time – and it's only painful if you believe otherwise.

Life is like a river, the moving clouds teach me, this evening after milking. Always moving. Always flowing. It may change slowly – but change it will.

18 September 2012

Waking up at 6 a.m. to do the milking – inky darkness and so windy outside that opening the door is like stepping into a river. But the house is filled with the smell of baking bread, and it somehow makes it all better. Thank goodness for the bread machine with a timer!

Rich's operation has been postponed. We don't know when it will happen now. Apparently this could go on for ages – the operation getting scheduled and cancelled, scheduled and cancelled. I'm trying to stay calm with the whole thing, as this country's National Health Service is so different from what I was used to in the USA.

While I was waiting nervously for news, there was a very lovely shaft of light, a bit of magical luck – we've won an award for our kefir! Janey Lee Grace, presenter on BBC Radio 2, author and expert on natural products, has awarded us her Platinum Award 2012. We get a platinum medallion to put on the website. I've printed out a paper version and put it in a frame by the front door, and I smile every time I go in or out.

A much-needed ray of sunshine in these dark days. Janey Lee Grace is such an inspiration, an amazing woman! She asked me whether I ever put the kefir into the soap. Interesting question! I wonder if it would work? Haven't got the time or energy to experiment with it at the moment, though.

11 November 2012

No news yet on Rich's operation, but an exciting turn for the business – in the wake of the Platinum Award from Janey Lee Grace, the *Daily Mail* national newspaper contacted us and asked if they could review our soap! They were doing an article about natural alternatives to household items that contain chemicals. But the soap would have to arrive in London by the following morning to make the deadline for the story.

Of course, we said yes and quickly packed up a box to send, and called the courier. But the courier didn't come. Finally, at 2 p.m., fighting panic, I phoned the central office. They said the driver was on his way. By 5 p.m. it seemed clear that there was a problem.

I was ready to get in the car myself and make the four-hour trip to drive the soap to the newspaper offices – I wasn't going to miss this opportunity! I rang the lovely girl at the front desk one last time, car keys in my hand, and told her the whole story. She told me that somehow the regular driver had gone missing.

But she rang a special driver, who showed up in the yard, in his own car, at 6:30 p.m. – with just enough time to get the box to the central depot before 7:30 p.m. We packed the small box into the boot of his car, and I stood in the yard and waved him away, feeling like I was watching a child go off to the first day of school. Fingers crossed...

14 November 2012

Wow, amazing, I can't believe it! Rushed to the local shop first thing this morning to buy the *Daily Mail* and flipped with trembling fingers to the article – where our soap was being reviewed – and they gave us nine out of 10! The highest score for any natural product. And our competitor, Pears Soap, only got two out of 10. Giddy and spinning around the kitchen – don't know what to do with myself!

The review says, *'Chuckling Goat Oatmeal & Honey Soap: You could eat every ingredient: goat's milk, which is anti-inflammatory; natural oils; grapefruit seed extract; honey and oatmeal. There's a subtle sweet smell, and the oatmeal gently scrubs your hands. This soap has a soft, creamy lather. My hands were left clean, but not over-dry. 9/10.'* Yippee! Must phone my mom.

4 December 2012

Still no news on Rich's op, but more exciting news for the business – we also got written up in the Welsh press. Here's what the *Western Mail* had to say about our soap:

'A little-known, natural hand-made soap made by a Welsh farming couple has just trumped and unseated cosmetics classic Pears Soap in a national newspaper review. Chuckling Goat Soap, made in Llandysul, was rated nine out of 10 against the traditional product, which only scored a two.'

Amazing!! Our lovely local shop, Hoffnant Londis, is stocking the soap and has put a little cut-out of the article next to the display. Everyone's been really lovely about it – we're feeling quite the local celebs! People who read the article, or saw us on the telly, are knocking on the door, asking for the soap and skin cream.

Astonished to discover how many people are desperate for a natural solution to eczema or psoriasis or rosacea. Traditional medicine just doesn't have much to offer, except the nasty steroid creams that thin your skin – and you're warned not to use those for longer than two weeks. At the end of that time, your skin is more delicate than before, you have to stop using the cream, and you've nothing to turn to. Worse off than ever!

Eczema is a horrible thing, especially for parents who have to watch their children suffering. There's a woman in the village here with two adorable little girls, one of whom has eczema so bad that her skin comes off on the sheets at night, and she wakes up with her pillow covered in blood. So heartbreaking, but now I can help her.

I think of that little girl when I'm making my soaps and skin creams, stirring the big pots on the stove in the farmhouse kitchen. It's simply miraculous to me that the goat's milk can help and heal so powerfully, and I'm so fortunate to be able to make things with it that can do some good! A wonderful feeling, to think that I'm actually accomplishing something in the world that can help someone... after so very many years of lots of smoke and noise and not accomplishing much of anything at all.

24 December 2012

There's a very lovely ancient tradition which holds that on Christmas Eve, at midnight, animals are given the power of speech. I've even heard it said that all the animals then sing songs of praise.

Walking into the warm barn – away from the icy, windy dark outside – it's easy to believe this lovely story. I look into the slender faces of my familiar, much-loved goats, with their dark eyes and knowing expressions, and I can easily imagine them opening their mouths to sing at midnight.

Glenda, Wandi, Patsi, Juliette – I know them all by name, and I can tell them apart, as identical as they might look to a stranger. I can imagine just how each of their voices might sound, raised in the choir. Juliette rears up her hind legs to have her cheek scratched – just there, by the hinge of her jaw – and to rub her head lovingly against my shoulder.

Coming here twice a day, to milk and to commune with these lovely animals, has taught me a thing or two about miracles. The goats have taught me about dedication, and patience, and discipline. Waking up at 6 a.m. on a freezing morning and going outside sounds like a punishment when I'm wrapped in my duvet. But as soon as I haul myself up and out, and into the barn, I realize the truth of it – coming here is my reward. The teaching really is in the practice – putting my hands on the goats, tending them and receiving the healing milk that they give me, is all I need to know of magic.

The Christian tradition holds that the king is born in midwinter. The pagan tradition too speaks of rebirth in the time of darkness. It's a principle as old as man, when we were frightened and crouching in the caves, waiting for the light to return. Peasants have milked goats for as long as humans have been around, and I follow this time-honoured tradition with gratitude now, as the warm streams of milk hit my pail in a fragmented melody.

In that song, I can hear everything I need to know about rebirth. These goats are pregnant in the darkness, gestating new life. In the spring, the kids will be born, and the milk will be freshened. The life force dies back and blossoms up again. New life. It's a miracle that we few – who are lucky enough to tend the farm – learn over again with our hands and feet, arms and eyes and hearts, every year without fail.

Christmas Eve – in the darkness – the goats and I wait together in the silence. We wait for the rebirth that is certain. It's certain as life, certain as breath, as certain as the knowledge that someday, spring will come again, and light will return to the world.

On the farm, there's a rhythm to the year. I never really understood the lyrics of the song *'Turn! Turn! Turn!'* by The Byrds – okay, originally a verse from the Book of Ecclesiastes – *'For every thing there's a season, and a time to every purpose under heaven.'* But it's true on the farm, and we live our life by it. Not because it's pretty, or romantic, but because the turning of the seasons demands it.

In the spring, the grass grows, and that's when the young animals are born – giving them the best chance of survival. For us that means kidding and lambing, baby goats to tend and feed, new milkers to be milked – incredibly busy!

Summer for us is all about the hay – cutting it, making it, turning it, baling it, getting it into the shed and stacked. The hay is what feeds our animals all year round, and a failure to get the hay in is a blow that cuts at the very heart of the farm. The hay is the top priority, and all hands are expected to turn out at a moment's notice to get it in if it looks like rain. We've worked well into the night at times, struggling to get the bales stacked under shelter before they're ruined by the constantly threatening damp.

Autumn is about harvest and preparing for the winter – battening down the hatches, preparing the barns for winter storms, cutting up and stacking the firewood that we'll depend on when it's freezing and slashing with icy rain.

And the winter? Then, we're quiet. Dormant – like the trees and the grass outside. We light the wood burner and settle in for that 'long winter's nap'. There are the holidays to enjoy and food to eat, friends to catch up with – the people we lost track of during the frantic rush of spring and summer. We go walking in the woodlands and cut evergreens and holly for the Christmas display.

And then there's the delicious time where I find myself now. Preparing for the New Year. The Christmas decorations have come down and been packed away, leaving dusty expanses of mantel, shelf, windowsill. And I find myself seized by the urge to clean, throw away, dust, discard. Freshen. Lighten. Make new choices.

This, I guess, is what they mean by spring cleaning. But for me, the impulse strikes now, when everything outside is slow and cold. More of a 'New Year's cleaning'.

There's a pulse to biological life – living things move in and out, like a breath. The period of activity is followed by a period of inactivity. A heart beats in its two-part rhythm. Lungs expand and contract. The sun rises and sets. Animals are born and die.

One of the things I remember about living in the city was the absence of any sort of pulse. Because you could go on all night and all year round, people did. There was more of a straight line right across – 24 hours! Open all night! Work harder and faster! – rather than the rising and falling sine curve of a natural pulse.

But preparing for the New Year is gathering in before launching out again into the spring, a resting and repairing, a looking around to see what needs fixing and changing for the year ahead. What needs a lick of paint? Do the kitchen worktops need fixing? Replacing?

Mine do. I want to paint them a cream colour, I think, and light sage green – the colour of new grass. Rich's operation has been scheduled and postponed yet again – we're looking for ways to keep ourselves from going mad with the up-and-down cycle of disappointment and dread... redecorating the kitchen seems as good a way as any!

2 January 2013

Unbelievably, there's yet another newspaper story about us! This one in the *Cambrian News*. 'Family's Passion Reaps Rewards: A couple from Brynhoffnant who bought some goats to use their milk to help cure their son of eczema and asthma have turned their passion into an award-winning small business.'

The business is booming on the back of all this lovely publicity – the phones are ringing and the orders are pouring in. We're still making a loss, but not as much of one! It seems as if this could actually work, if we can just catch a break, and stop getting hammered with disaster. Now if we could just get Rich's operation scheduled, done, dusted and behind us. The dread and anticipation hangs over us like a black cloud, dimming the pleasure of even the most exciting news.

24 February 2013

Rich had his second operation on Friday. After waiting for such a long time, in the end things moved very rapidly, the days sliding like beads down a string. The operation was moved forward by five days, so it came quite abruptly.

I drove him to hospital on Thursday, and stayed with him while he got settled in. We'd packed a bag for him at home, with tracksuit bottoms, Crocs to wear in the hospital halls and clean T-shirts. All hopeful items, because we knew he wouldn't be wearing anything but a hospital gown for a long, long time.

I had to leave, finally, to go home and do the milking. I bit my lip and found my eyes welling with tears as I walked quickly down the long hall, heading back to the car park. I hate leaving him in there on his own.

Friday came, and Rich texted me to say he was going in first thing. I finished the morning milking and headed to the hospital again – one hour and 25 minutes it takes, door to door. By now, our second time around, I know the route exactly. I set my laptop up in the hospital café, phoned the head nurse and gave her my mobile number, bought a coffee and waited. And waited.

It was nearly six hours later when I gave up any hope of them calling me. I walked back up to the ward. He was in recovery, they said, and I couldn't go in. I knew where recovery was, though, from the last time, and I walked there and knocked on the door.

I could see Rich on the table, very pale but awake, and waved at him past the orderly's shoulder. The orderly took pity on me, 20 minutes later, and smuggled me into the recovery room, where I heard the story from the nurse of Rich coming out of sedation thrashing wildly, maddened with pain because they'd put the epidural in the wrong place. He was dopey and groggy – which was only to be expected.

Next day, when I went in, it was to hear that he'd had an unbelievably bad night – his intestine had stopped working, stopped making its rhythmic contractions of peristalsis, and, as a result, he vomited, straining the new wound that stripes down his front, from his breast bone to his pubic bone.

No infection, no fever, no sepsis, the perky blonde nurse told me. They X-rayed him and everything was fine.

Everything except his intestine, which – insulted and manhandled – had sulkily gone to sleep and now refused to move. It should 'wake up' tomorrow, they said. Or perhaps the next day. In the meantime, they'd put a tube down his nose to drain his stomach.

I stared at her, trying to take it in.

She smiled reassuringly and said, 'It *will* wake up.'

I hope so.

It occurs to me that there isn't a lot we can do about the body if the body refuses to cooperate. You can't *make* it do anything. You can only create the conditions in which it could possibly happen – and then hope that it does.

Rich's insides, lying still when they need to be moving and pulsing. There's no alternative to that. You can't live, if your intestine refuses to move.

He wasn't pale, oddly – his face was pink, a better colour than it has been for a long time. We didn't talk much – I just held his hand.

27 February 2013

Nearly a week now, and Rich's insides are still lying unmoving, inert. The day before when I went in he was a little brighter – yesterday, he frightened me. So tired, he seemed to have just given up. I wanted to tell him to fight, but I couldn't, he just seemed so weary.

I came home and phoned his brother, frantic with worry: 'We have to get him into a private room. He hasn't eaten or slept in a week, and the man next to him screams and cries and gibbers non-stop. It's like hell. We have to get him out of there.'

We talked, worrying it round in circles. What could we do? I resolved to try to throw money at the problem – maybe it would help?

Monday on the way to the hospital my front tyre dissolved in a rush of canvas. When I called the roadside assistance company, and they took me to the garage, it emerged that both front tyres were completely bald. Had I driven another two minutes onto the motorway, the tyres might have caused a fatal crash, exploding when I was going at top speed.

I never check the tyres, it's always Rich's job. But of course Rich isn't here. What's the lesson here, I wondered? Is it that I have to do everything myself again, like when I was a single mom? I felt angry that Rich had sent me out onto the roads in a car that was dangerous. But of course I couldn't be angry at him, lying there defeated and – it seems – so close to death himself.

That night, I lay in bed with my eyes stinging, staring at the ceiling. Still wondering. What's the lesson here? Is there one? If there were a lesson, what would it be?

Not 'What if' said a voice in my head. 'What *is*.' I didn't crash. I could have, and I might have. But I didn't.

Suffering is mental. I can see that. I learned that during my nine-and-a-half-hour marathon to get to the hospital and home, by way of two new tyres. Each part, in itself, was okay.

Sitting in the hospital coffee shop waiting for the breakdown company to arrive. Driving. At least I was warm and dry. Even finally reaching the hospital after six and a half hours on the road, to be told that I'd have to wait another half-hour because visiting time hadn't yet begun. I could stand propped up in the hall; it wasn't so bad. The suffering is only bad when you start to let it stack up. The experience of each moment – moment to moment – is not so bad.

And another gift of this hard time – freedom from fear. I'm no longer afraid of hospitals, of tyres blowing out, of strangers screaming in the night, of my husband lying near death and me unable to help. I've seen all these things, and I can handle them. I'm still here. Freedom from fear. The final gift of going all the way down to the bottom.

When it was time to leave today, I suddenly felt as if Rich might simply drift away while I was gone.

'Look at me,' I said. 'I want you to promise me that when I come back tomorrow, you'll still be here.'

He looked quite shifty and wouldn't quite meet my eyes.

'I can't promise that,' he said.

'You promise,' I insisted. 'You look into my eyes and promise me.'

In the end, he promised. Later, he told me this: he dreamed that night that he'd been in a train crash. And in the dream, it seemed imperative that he get away from the train. There was a bright white light. In real life, apparently, he got up and pulled all his drips out, and started wandering across the ward. The nurse came to get him – in real life, or in his dream? Hard to tell – and said to him, 'Where are you going?'

'You're the one who works here; you're supposed to know where I'm going,' he replied.

'You need to make up your mind where you want to go,' she said.

'I promised,' he said. 'I'd better go back.'

And she helped him back into bed. When he told me this story, I had the strangest feeling that if we looked around the ward for that nurse, we wouldn't find her.

28 February 2013

Finally, good news today! After more than a week, the surgeon got Rich's intestine moving again – apparently by reaching his hand through the incision and down into Rich's insides, right there on the hospital bed in the ward. The head nurse told me that he's better, that he's moving back towards life.

Thank God. Thank God.

3 March 2013

I've just worked out why it matters to keep things cleaned up. I've always known that I should. Obviously it's good to be tidy, and so on. But I always did it with a certain amount of resentment, as if I was completing a chore for the approval of someone who'd look over my shoulder. And if I was too busy, or too tired, then I didn't bother, and the mess would mount up.

This morning I woke at 6 a.m., got up and started cleaning the bedroom.

Our bedroom is the last room of the house to receive any attention. When I moved in with my two children, we had to make room for all of us. So I thought it should be my gift to Rich's girls that they would get all-new grown-up bedrooms that they could design themselves. I brought home stacks of magazines, and they flipped through and picked out the colours and ideas that they liked. Then they each got a budget, and we went shopping for carpets, paint, blinds, furniture.

Ceris chose a dramatic scarlet wall, with black trimmings and white carpet. Elly went for a wooden floor, apple-green wall and a cityscape in her room. I thought both the results were gorgeous, and the excitement of the decorating carried us through what might have been a sticky period of new people and children intruding on their dad's turf, time and attention.

My two got their own rooms, as well. Benji's has each wall painted a different shade of tractor colour. Joli's has photographs on the ceiling, a squashy leather couch and gold walls. But our room – Rich's and mine – still has the dingy brown carpet and tattered heavy brown curtains that were there when I moved in. And, I suspect, when he moved in 15 years ago, along with his parents, his two girls and his first wife! It's filled with heavy antique wooden furniture, too ponderous to move easily to clean.

But it has a stunning view of the sea, and we've been so happy there that fresh paint and carpet seems the least of our concerns. The children have their rooms; the kitchen has been tidied, and there's new furniture in the lounge. But we've been so busy in the past five years, getting settled into the house, getting married, getting the goats going, setting up a business, that we fall into bed, into each other's arms, exhausted at the end of each day, barn clothes dropped in a dusty pile.

Decorating has just never been high on the list. Or cleaning, for that matter, aside from general hygiene and laundry in, laundry out. But this morning I woke up and started clearing surfaces, emptying trash, dusting. I could suddenly see that the problem with clutter is that it gives the illusion of permanence. It gives 'STUFF' the upper hand.

Really, it's not the stuff that's in control. It's not the material things that matter – it's the idea. If I have the idea of cleanliness, the matter falls into line. The stuff follows along obediently. Stuff – matter – makes a good servant but a poor master. And if I let everything get cluttered and dusty, I feel so bowed down by the weight of it that I buy into the illusion that it's solid.

And of course, it isn't.

That's the secret key that I've worked out during this most horrific of all weeks. When Rich lay in his hospital bed with his intestine inert, hovering between life and death; when my tyres ruptured on the way to the hospital; when the water system packed in and we had to drag buckets of water to each goat; when Benji had chicken pox and then a stomach virus and had to be picked up from school immediately as an emergency.

Rhys called me 'Calamity Jane' – a tag I categorically deny. I may have had lesson after lesson stacked up this week, but here's what I learned:

Light can be both wave and particle – and so can we. I actually think that awareness, or consciousness, is the mechanism that turns waves into particles. It's waves until it hits our consciousness. And then we translate the energy into particles – or stuff. Like play dough being squeezed through a shaped tube, it comes out in whatever shape you give it.

Reality isn't actually dense. And things aren't as solid as they appear. We know this, because the scientists tell us so. The wooden table that looks so solid – or the clutter on the dresser – is really just vibrating particles, with space in between. The weight of matter is an illusion.

It's a convincing illusion, to be sure. And letting things get cluttered and dirty – letting the stuff take over – makes the illusion even more convincing.

But really, reality is more like Jaron Lanier's original virtual reality game than I knew. Our brains are the controller – we project our beliefs onto the outside world, and they come into being. A good reason to be very careful about what beliefs you're carrying around – because you're constantly bringing them into being.

5 March 2013

Rich is coming home today! He's been in hospital for nine days – this is the tenth. Thinking back on it, I realize that we almost lost him.

There was that long, long time when he was vacant – when his eyes weren't his eyes, when he was staring straight ahead, conscious but not present. When his insides were inert, still, not moving. When I wanted to urge him to fight, to come back to me – but there was no-one to urge.

It was almost like he was a mist, in the shape of a man. In any case, he's come back to me – to us – now. Grumpy, tired, demanding jelly babies and beer, but himself. Thank God for that. A man, not just a mist in the shape of a man.

And I've learned... what have I learned? I think it's about created suffering. My father told me something about a bear. If you throw a flaming log at a bear, it'll clutch the burning wood to its own chest. That's because clutching is a bear's defence mechanism – that's how it kills things. And it can't do anything else, even if that natural response is harming it. We're like that. We're like a bear, clutching the burning log to ourselves. There's suffering, sure, but we create more suffering than we need to, by focusing on the 'what if' instead of the 'what is'.

Rich is coming home, and I could be spending all my time panicking about what happens if he has an emergency once he gets here, worrying about how long it'll take him to recover, fretting about how I'll manage to run the farm on my own during the long months of his convalescence.

But all of that is 'what *if*'. Instead of 'what *is*'.

So, what is?

I'm back in my kitchen – my beautiful apple-green kitchen, with its long view of the sea and the hills and the trees on the other side of the valley. Outside, the goats wait for me, their breaths misting in the cold morning air, fragrant with clean straw and hay, warm silky flanks and goat's milk waiting to hit the churns in steaming streams. Healing lotions and potions to make. Family to love. Work to do. The farm itself, surrounding me like a pair of arms. These are the things I cling to, the things that keep me strong. And I need to be strong.

Rich is now installed on the couch. Still gaunt, grey, hunched over and very tired – and a literal shadow of his former hay-bale-swinging self – but home. He's always been terrifically tough, a farmer who thrives on being outside in any weather.

Just as well, because any lesser man probably would have just given up and died after what he's been through. But he didn't. He survived. His 25-cm- (10-inch-) long abdominal incision was covered with a long, long bandage right down his mid-line, which we were instructed not to remove for a week.

On his third day home, the bandage looked so grim – sort of wet and soggy – that Rich and I thought it needed to be replaced. We clearly weren't going to be able to wait for an entire week.

One of the many wonderful things about the UK is that the NHS has what they call district nurses, who actually make house calls and care for you in your home. To an American like myself, this is amazing!

So we contacted the district nurse and explained the situation. She came out to the farm, washed her hands, and spread out the field pack with clean surgical dressings. I stood by and watched, gripping the arm of the sofa, in case I felt wobbly. It seemed like a very long moment, as the nurse carefully peeled the bandage away.

What I saw horrified me. Rich couldn't look down and see his own incision very well, and he was looking at my face – so I tried to keep my expression calm and blank. But I wanted to scream. I bit my tongue firmly, so I wouldn't make a noise.

Instead of a neatly healing wound, there were red holes in the incision, gaping like little red wet mouths.

Silently, the nurse swabbed the wound, and put the swab into a packet to send away for testing. She put iodine patches over the worst of the red holes and taped a clean new bandage down the length of Rich's torso. I made her a cup of coffee, and we talked about inconsequential things. None of us mentioned what we'd just seen.

A different district nurse came to the house the next day, to re-dress the wound. There wasn't any change – although the little red mouths seemed a little deeper. By the next day, the results of the test had come back. It was the worst possible news – MRSA. Rich's abdominal incision was infected with an antibiotic-resistant superbug.

I remember hearing the nurse say the words, and feeling that my knees might give way. Everything tilted a bit, and my vision went grainy. And then I put my hand down on the arm of the couch, to steady myself, and tried to concentrate on the rest of what she was saying.

Reading headlines in the newspaper about the existence of bacteria that cannot be treated with antibiotics is one thing. Hearing that someone you love has that type of infection is something different.

I thought, stupidly, 'This can't be happening.' And then I started asking questions. What did it mean, exactly? And what could we do about it?

What it meant, apparently, was that Rich's wound had been colonized with MRSA bacteria, also known as 'flesh-eating' bacteria. So, instead of the wound healing, the bacteria were literally eating new holes in the wound, which were growing deeper by the day.

What could we do? Very little. All of the creams and injections available were based on antibiotics – and MRSA is resistant to antibiotics.

In the Western world, our misuse – and overuse – of antibiotics means that we've now succeeded in killing off the weaker strains of bacteria, leaving the more virulent ones to breed and become resistant to our medicines. And out of that chemical stew, which we created, has arisen a new monster – a bacterial strain that we no longer have the tools to fight. It has out-evolved us, outsmarted our best scientists.

We've created a nightmare superbug, one that was, at that very moment, sitting in my lounge, on my sofa, infesting my husband. And there wasn't a damn thing we could do about it. We were weapon-less, defenceless. Without antibiotics, the doctors have nothing to offer.

The district nurse continued to come every day, to pull the long bandage off, measure the little holes in the wound with a tiny ruler that was included in the field pack they distribute for this purpose, and re-pack the wound with sterilized seaweed.

The purpose of the seaweed was to keep the wound open, so that it would heal up from the bottom. The last thing you want in a situation like this is for the wound to heal over the top, with the infection trapped inside.

Rich rose to the occasion, as he always does, joking with the nurse as she made her measurements and poked the seaweed – which looked like tiny spun fibres of insulation material – down into the holes in the wound with a minute sterile probe. She put a fresh bandage over the top – a long one, more than 30cm (1 foot)

in length – and taped it down. We were all relieved, I think, when the wound was out of sight.

Each day, she would put a new iodine patch over the worst of the holes, hoping it would dry up the infection. A new gauze dressing, new tape holding it down. Rich's skin grew red and raw from the place where the tape was pulled off, day after day.

And then we began the waiting. Waiting for what, I wasn't exactly sure. But what else could we do?

14 March 2013

Rich has still been taking the antibiotics. Even though we know that the MRSA is resistant, it feels wrong to just sit by and do nothing. But they have been making him nauseous, and when he throws up, it wrenches the entire incision open again. The doctor has now recommended that he stop taking them altogether.

Yesterday he came off the antibiotics and only felt nauseous once. I peeled and pounded up one root of fresh ginger, poured boiling water over it, added the juice of half a lemon and some organic demerara sugar and topped it off with soda water. I gave this concoction to Rich to drink. He liked it, and it seemed to settle his stomach. At least he didn't retch again – celebrate the small victories!

I'm not normally a fan of 'natural' remedies – they always seems slightly hippie-style to me, and ineffective. I'm not interested in things that don't work. I'd much rather just take a pill and get it over with. But this time, I don't have much choice. And at least making up a natural remedy gives me something to do, and makes me feel useful. We'll see how we get on today.

The bad news is that Rich was violently ill again last night. I was hoping that it was the antibiotics that had been making him sick to his stomach, but he still seems to feel nauseous without them. I made him another fresh ginger drink – it seems to be the only thing I have to offer... I hate feeling so helpless!

I've been thinking and thinking about MRSA and it occurs to me that maybe part of the problem is the aggressive language we've been using around this whole infection thing: phrases like, 'We're going to beat it', 'We're fighting it' or 'We're going to kill the bad bacteria.' They're all violent metaphors.

In money terms that aggression looks like this: I have something to sell. You offer me less than it's worth. We haggle. I say it's great; you say it's rubbish. You're knocking it down, destroying it in my eyes and yours, trying to make it worth less. We try to buy everything for the lowest possible price. It's quite nasty, that model, when you think about it.

It's the opposite of giving a gift, where you offer your very best and don't count the cost. It's also the opposite of the way a female goat suckles a kid – she doesn't give it just a bit of milk – it all flows out! The let-down reflex of nature is all about abundant generosity, not hold-back, where we try to drive each other down.

In medical terms that aggression looks like pointing a medical gun – antibiotics (anti-life, literally!) – at little tiny things we can't see, and trying to kill as many of them as possible. Unsurprisingly, this hasn't worked very well. You can kill a lot of them, but the leftover ones that escape (and some will always escape!) mutate and turn into your worst nightmare monster – a resistant superbug.

So maybe, just maybe, we're thinking about this all wrong. Maybe we don't need to 'fight' this. Maybe fighting is the wrong way to go about it. Maybe we just need to dance it into the light.

I've put the business on hold for the moment. I don't seem to be able to cope with the everyday demands of filling orders and selling things, when I want to be concentrating all of my energy on Rich.

And if we're going to find a solution to this, it's going to have to be outside the box, since there are no workable solutions inside the box. For me to come up with that solution, I'm going to have to completely change the way I'm thinking – not just about Rich, not just about the MRSA, but about everything. About the business, as well.

I have to walk the talk, whatever that means. I've got to shift the paradigm completely, inside my head, as well as in the outside world.

I've no idea what I'm talking about! I think I may be losing the plot a bit. So do my family, by the way – they've insisted that I go and see my GP, because they think I'm cracking up. I'm not depressed exactly – more on an adrenaline high. My GP checked me over and said he thought I was having a normal stress reaction to crisis.

Don't know about 'normal'. What is normal, in a situation like this one? It does feel like I'm running on overdrive at the moment. But if overdrive is how this problem will be solved, then so be it!

It just feels like I have to do *everything* differently. As Einstein said, a problem can't be solved on the same level it was created. So how to take everything to a different level, where it *can* be solved? What would that different level look like? How would it work?

Think, think, think! I tell myself.

Well, for one thing, it wouldn't be aggressive. It would be – I don't know – like bees. Like the way bees pollinate flowers – they don't negotiate, pollen grain for pollen grain. Bees and flowers deal in abundance. Because this is the way the natural world works – more pollen, more flowers, more honey, more bees. More for everyone, not less.

It's the way biology works – the abundance of let-down, not the stinginess of hold-back. Only human beings practise hold-back. And it hasn't worked very well for us.

What would the generosity of let-down look like, if it was practised out in the business world? Maybe, instead of money, we use a 'Golden Ticket' system. Magic, like Willy Wonka.

We ask our customers to do one random good deed – not a big one, just any little thing to make the world a better place. Pay the toll for the person behind you. Give someone a gift they're not expecting. Chase after the little old lady who left her cash card in the machine, just anything... and then they can post their good deed on our Facebook page. At the end of the week, we pick out one good deed and send the winner a basket of our goodies – milk, kefir, soap and skin cream.

So, for the moment, while the business is on pause, I'm not going to use money. I'm not going to sell things. I'm not going to trade in that aggressive paradigm – not in any way. I'm in the market for magic, miracles and light at the moment. That's what I need to save Rich – a miracle. So that's what I want. So you can't buy our products for cash just at the moment. You can only purchase them for good deeds, information and ideas.

Later... Astonishing results!

Suddenly our Facebook page has become a clearing house for good deeds, well-wishers and creative ideas about alternative therapies. I love logging onto it. I feel absolutely embraced by people I've never met – people who are sending us ideas and remedies, giving us the benefit of their wisdom and research.

One of our first Golden Ticket winners sent me a great article about the effects of blue light on MRSA, with science that shows that it works. I've ordered my blue light home-use gizmo, and am now waiting with bated breath for it to arrive. We've been getting so much support from customers and friends, people who have ideas about alternative treatments and ways to heal MRSA. Maybe one of the answers will be the one that works, the one we need?

4 April 2013

Good news. We definitely seem to be winning the battle of the incision – it's drying up and beginning to heal properly. The nurse is pleased and considering cutting back her visits to every other day.

7 April 2013

Rich's incision continues to heal well – it's dry and closing nicely. I put a Manuka honey-infused dressing on the wound when we re-dressed it after his bath. But he's still so tired, and pale, and weak... and still feeling very nauseous morning and night. How best to support his system now? Does he still have MRSA in his body, even though the wound is healing nicely?

My guess is that he does – even though we can't really know for sure, because the only way to test is to swab the wound and it's now so healed that there's nothing to swab. But he just still doesn't seem *right* to me. And it seems too much to expect that such a potent bacteria would be completely gone from his system.

Even though he's still so weak, Rich wanted to go shopping for a new bed. It's a strange time because he spends most of the day on the couch, but he can get up from time to time. I was worried that the trip would be too much for him – we've only been out once since he came out of hospital, to have lunch with some old friends – but he insisted, and so we set out. We went straight into the shop, bought the bed and came straight home again, but the effort still exhausted him hugely, and he's still tired today.

One of our customers sent me an article about a powerful combination of essential oils that was used during the Middle Ages. It's been shown in modern studies to kill viruses and bacteria, including MRSA and E. coli. I want to do some research... why are essential oils bio-active against viruses, when most of conventional medicine isn't? What combination would work? Can I make it here on my kitchen table, and if I do, will it work on Rich?

Rich wants to stick to the goat's milk kefir, which we make ourselves and sell, and the anti-inflammatory herb mix that I was giving him before the surgery. It's a combination of herbs recommended to me by a medical herbalist friend who came to stay with us and help on the farm. I brew it up in a big saucepan, with some Manuka honey in it.

Cooled, he can sip on it and it worked really well when his joints were achy and painful before the surgery. He seems better, the wound looks better, but I don't know, it still just doesn't seem right.

10 April 2013

Today is our third wedding anniversary. And for the first time in weeks, Rich seems better. This morning, as I was milking the goats, I was startled to see a face pop into the milking parlour –

it was Rich! It just goes to show what a long time it's been since he was outside – and he used to *live* outside. Never happier than when he was on his tractor, mowing the hay.

These days he's looking a bit more like an apostle – pale and thinned-down – than a pirate, which is how he used to look! But it was still lovely to see him outdoors.

He's been able to do a few projects around the place as well – he got the water and sewerage connected to our lovely caravan (which we call the Treehouse because when you're in it all you can see is treetops), so he actually did a lot of work. Still feeling a bit nauseous, but the incision has healed so well that it scarcely needs a bandage.

I received the ingredients for my magic essential oil mix today. In the post. Isn't it funny that the only things that seem to work against viruses are natural? Manuka honey, and this combo of essential oils – could it possibly work for us? Can't wait to try it!

Rich prefers a shower to a bath – he's too tall to fit comfortably into our little bathtub – so I think I'll blend up my own combination of the oils and give him a footbath with it in front of the telly. At least it smells nice – and it can't hurt, let's face it. He'll hate it – he loathes being fussed over! But I'm going to insist anyway. I have hope that these essential oils will drive the MRSA away for good.

24 April 2013

Rich *was* better – so much better. The incision was clean, and dry, and looked almost completely healed – just like a scar, really. But then we went into the hospital for a check-up. The surgeon opened the wound and looked at it, and then dressed it again without the honey, in just a brief bandage with no waterproofing. The next day there were two bright red patches – and the day after that they'd burst open again. Re-infected with MRSA! I can't believe it.

He's so much worse now. I was furious with the nurses, who refused to put the Manuka honey dressing on the wound – why, why, when there's so much research indicating that medical honey works on MRSA? That it keeps the bacteria from becoming resistant to antibiotics?

We'd bought and paid for our own surgical bandages infused with sterile Manuka honey, and even brought with us an article from the NHS website – which I'd printed and actually laminated – all about the benefits of medical honey. And still the nurses refused to use the bandages, because they're 'not on the protocol list'. One nurse told me they're not on the list because they're too expensive. Yet even when I buy my own, they won't use them.

So, now we're back to square one – a new and frightening gaping hole in the wound, growing ever deeper and closer to Rich's vital organs. This time the wound has to be packed and dressed three times a day. The nurse can only come once a day, so that leaves the other two times to me. I never trained as a nurse, but it doesn't seem to matter – I've figured out by now that you can do whatever you have to.

Rich sits on the sofa, and I wash my hands and then spread out everything we need on the table by the fire. The field packs they've given us have everything in them – a rubber apron, rubber gloves, clean gauze, washes, wipes. We have packs of the seaweed and the probe that the nurse used. There's even a little trash bag included.

I look into Rich's eyes, and smile. He smiles back at me. Even now, he jokes to keep my spirits up. It breaks my heart. He sets his teeth, nods at me and I pull the long, long bandage off. He winces as the tape tears at his ravaged skin. The holes are deeper, I'm sure of it. Today I'll call the NHS and ask about medical maggots – maybe they will help.

I put the little plastic probe into the deepest hole, pull it out and measure it. It's deeper again. It doesn't seem to hurt Rich when I put the probe in, or at least if it does, he never shows it. I pack the seaweed into the holes with the probe, and cover it up again. Clean gauze dressing, strapped down with clean tape.

Relief – we're finished again for another few hours.

Rich is getting very ill now. The infection finally seems to be wearing him down. He spends more time in bed.

I made soap today – lemon and mint, to try to raise my spirits. Even when I'm at my lowest, making the soap, inhaling the beautiful scents of the aromatherapy oils, makes me feel better....

Soon, I'll have to change Rich's bandage again. Life, it seems, is a very heavy business indeed. And yet, when I close my eyes in the middle of milking, emerging from the beating of the milk machine I hear in my head the beginning of Beethoven's Ninth – that final, joyous, overcoming shout. I felt today a sudden sense of space, of speeding over the landscape, of pouring and dipping and shifting, of flying over the sea, of the land rippling under me and out as far as I could see.

And from that place – that weightless, groundless place – I felt that I was dislocated from time, and that I could see all the lives of all the people living now, and the ones who've lived before, all spread out in a marvellous tapestry of forests and streams and oceans. And I was flying over all of it, amazingly free.

My particular pain, over this particular circumstance, was only one bit of a whole. A larger, much larger, and much more wonderful whole. If I close my eyes, I can still feel the vertigo of coming unstuck from my own particular suffering, and soaring over the whole scintillating landscape, the laughter of amazement coming out of my mouth.

Faith comes flooding back – that we will come out of this victorious, that although it seems impossible, we will win in the end. The weapons that we have – love, and light, and goat's milk, and honey and probiotics – will be enough. They will be.

They must be. They're all we've got.

26 April 2013

The nurse came this morning, looked at Rich's wound, and went pale. She said, very calmly, 'I think we need to call the doctor.'

The doctor came out – a young man. He looked at the wound and he too went pale. 'I haven't had any experience with something of this magnitude,' he said, as he quickly re-packed his bag. 'I think you need to contact the surgeon.'

He grabbed his bag, scurried out of the kitchen, slammed his car door and roared out of the drive. I was left speechless, looking after him. The nurse looked at me apologetically, and then she left as well.

The surgeon? I was supposed to contact the surgeon?

I would call the surgeon's secretary, and she would ask me why I was ringing. I would explain, and there would be a long silence on the other end of the phone.

Let's face it, the surgeon has already done his work. He operated. This is a post-operative infection – not something a surgeon can fix by operating again. And anyhow, Rich can't be readmitted to hospital. They screen you for MRSA before you're allowed in. And since they know for a fact that he's infected, they won't readmit him. He could pass the infection on to other patients, as MRSA is contagious.

I sat still at the kitchen table for a long time, admitting to myself the very real possibility that Rich might die on my sofa.

I felt as if I was looking at one of those ancient maps, where unexplored territories are inscribed with the words, 'Here Be Dragons'. It felt as if that was our location – beyond help, beyond knowledge, beyond expert advice. If the doctors, surgeons and nurses couldn't help us, who could? Who would advise us?

I thought about losing Rich, the one great love of my life. I was 41 when we met, with an entire lifetime of mistakes behind me.

I set my jaw and put my fist down on the table, very gently, so that I wouldn't disturb Rich. This *was not* going to be the way my happy ending finished. I'd not come through everything I'd come through, and worked this hard, and travelled halfway round the world to find this man, only to have him die on my sofa. This was *not* happening – not on *my* watch. Not while I had one breath left in my body to fight it.

I thought of my favourite saying, the one that I tell myself when things get very, very dark – which, in my dramatic and somewhat chequered life, they have frequently done! I call it the Toast of the Unrepentant Cowgirl. I came up with it while sitting on a gravestone, back in California, after a very bad day. It's best accompanied by a shot of straight tequila, and it goes something like this:

> *'One day, the world will knock me down*
> *and I will not get up again.*
> *But that day is not today*
> *you sons-a-bitches.*
> *Not today!'*

Not today.

I thought again about that combination of essential oils I'd mixed up in the soap room, the one that started out based on ancient research. My own modern variation on an old recipe. Would it work? Would it help? I'd no idea. But it couldn't hurt. And let's face it, I didn't have a lot to lose.

I put some of the oil mix into a bowl of warm water. Rich was wrapped completely up in the duvet. I got a clean washcloth out of the airing cupboard, took a deep breath, and fixed a smile on my face.

'We're going to try something different this morning,' I said.

Rich was too tired and weak to complain – probably just as well.

Taking one limb at a time out of his warm cocoon, dipping the washcloth into the oil-scented water and squeezing it dry, I gently washed down his arms and legs. A lovely fragrance spread through the air....

I wasn't brave enough to put the oil onto the wound itself – what if it burned? What if it stung him? What if it made it all worse? If it went wrong, it would be all my fault, and I couldn't cope with that possibility. So on the wound, I decided, I would just put more medical honey dressings.

As I worked, I thought about the time that we'd gone back to the surgeon for a check-up – on the visit where I believe Rich had become re-infected. The surgeon had given us a bit of information about MRSA. 'It colonizes all over your body,' he'd said. 'Every normal skin cell that you have is replaced with a copy of the MRSA.'

If that was the case, I thought now, no wonder it's so hard to clear the infection. You can clear the MRSA out of the wound all you like, but it'll constantly re-infect itself from the surrounding skin.

But what if I could knock back the numbers of the MRSA, by using this oil? I'd never kill them all, of course – there would be bacteria under his fingernails, in his hair, everywhere – but if I could just *reduce* the numbers of the pathogens.

And then... I suddenly thought about our kefir.

It's amazingly powerful, and its greatest power is that it *repopulates* the gut with good bacteria. It suddenly occurred to me that this was the missing piece of the puzzle: repopulation. It's no good just killing off the bad bacteria – they'll always regrow – what we needed to do was put some good bacteria in there, to repopulate.

Nature abhors a vacuum, right? It's always going to get filled with something. We needed to have allies in the microbiome. Get the good bacteria to come in and fill up the space, so that the bad bacteria couldn't take over again.

Kefir works in the gut that way. Would it work that way on the surface of the skin as well? I'd read that you could put kefir into face masks, and that it helps the skin. And again, I reasoned, it couldn't hurt.

Looking down at my semi-conscious husband, I knew that I'd nothing left to lose.

In the dairy we'd been working on an experimental version of kefir – hoping to develop a product that didn't rely so heavily on the goat's milk. As part of the process, we'd been working with coconuts. And since I'd no idea what I was doing – as usual! – we'd started out using coconut milk, instead of coconut water.

Coconut milk, as it turns out, is high in saturated fat, and isn't particularly great to drink. Coconut water, on the other hand, is a fantastic way to rehydrate your body and has loads of benefits that make it a perfect base for a probiotic drink.

But while I was working out the difference, we had kefir-ized a batch of coconut milk. It'd raised a heavy layer of fat, like on gravy. Disappointed, I'd tested the liquid underneath the layer of fat, finding it full of bits and not nice to drink. A failure.

Poking at the layer of congealed oil sitting on top, though, I realized that this was *probiotic* coconut oil. Coconut oil is good for your skin, in any case. I use it in the soap. It's also anti-viral. And this particular coconut oil, being probiotic, would be just the thing to repopulate good bacteria on the surface of the skin.

If any of my theories were right, of course. And if I wasn't absolutely barking insane. Which, at this point, seemed like a very real possibility.

I ran downstairs to get the failed-experiment probiotic coconut oil out of the fridge. 'What are you doing?' Rich asked, looking up at me blearily when I came back, out of breath but triumphantly clutching my experimental jar.

'Putting coconut kefir on you,' I said firmly, trying to sound as if I knew what I was doing.

'Oh,' he said, and went back to sleep.

I rubbed the probiotic coconut oil into as much of Rich's skin as I could reach – onto his torso, arms and legs, hands and feet and face. Whether it would help or not, who could tell? But at least I felt better, with something to do. And the oil was moisturizing and good for his skin, which had gone very dry during the infection.

30 April 2013

Rich has been very dopey, these past few days, fading in and out of an exhausted sleep. I've been carrying on with my new-found regimen – dropping the essential oil combination into a bowl of warm water (I used our big ceramic cake mixing bowl) and gently sponging Rich's limbs down with a clean washcloth dipped into the water. After that, I dry him off and then rub the kefir-ized coconut oil into his skin.

Then I curl up in bed next to him and we talk, facing each other on the pillow. He's often very cold, and has the duvet right up around his head, like a hood.

We've talked about crazy things – like the possibility of Rich and Benji making a rocket ship fuelled with kefir. Why not? We've talked about how Rich, wrapped in his duvet, is like a giant Daddy Butterfly in his cocoon – why are butterflies always considered to be female, anyhow? And about how someday I'll have a posh wet room installed where our grubby old bathroom is now, complete with an enormous bath tub, big enough for both of us to fit into, like the one we'd had in France on our honeymoon.

We've talked about how we'll go on a trip to Sardinia, to see how they keep their goats there, and about how someday we'll meet the Prince of Wales.

It all seems about as possible as Rich ever getting up out of bed.

I've kept on with the oil wash and the kefir rub, even though there seems little point; it's all I have and so I've grimly, stubbornly persisted.

The nurse has been over daily, to change Rich's dressing. She's finally given in to my incessant nagging and agreed to use the medical honey dressing. I think she pitied me, and thought it wouldn't make any difference anyway.

But then, one morning, she looked up at me with a surprised look on her face. I glanced over, rather hopelessly. I'd given up expecting anything in particular.

'I think it's... better?' she said cautiously.

I hurried over to look at the long incision down Rich's midline that I'd come to know so well. The two wet red holes, like angry mouths that refused to close – one right at his navel, the other a couple of inches higher. They looked – well, smaller. Drier, maybe? Not so angry.

'Do you think so?' I asked.

'It's a bit smaller today,' she said, peering closely at the plastic probe and double-checking it against the tiny ruler from the field pack. 'I'm almost sure of it.'

'Told you,' said Rich, from the pillow. 'There never was anything much wrong with me to start with.'

I punched him on the arm, very, very gently.

'You reckon not?'

'I reckon not,' he said, and grinned up at me.

4 May 2013

Today when the nurse came I was waiting expectantly, and walked her straight into the lounge. Rich was feeling better, and was sitting on the sofa. There was a different feel in the air – lighter, and happier. Something had shifted, I was sure of it.

The nurse pulled off the long dressing, and we all leaned in for a better look – the nurse and I peering in from either side, Rich looking down from the top. We all drew a breath in at the same time.

It *was* better. Definitely, absolutely better. Drier, smaller, lighter. Healing over. Pink, rather than red. Drawing in from the edges, it looked like a different wound.

I felt a rush of blood to my head so violent that I had to sit down.

'It's definitely healing, isn't it?' I asked the nurse.

'It's healing,' she confirmed.

I left the room and went upstairs into the bedroom, where I burst into tears – of relief, I guess. Or exhaustion. Hard to tell. I cried hard for about two minutes, then blew my nose and took myself back downstairs. The nurse was just packing up.

'I've taken another swab, just to be sure,' she said. 'We'll send it off and see what it says.'

6 May 2013

We're still waiting for the swab results, but in the meantime, Rich is rapidly regaining strength and colour. The wound is drying and healing; once on the mend, it has quickly shrunk in size until there's almost nothing left of it.

I feel that we've really turned the corner, but we've been down this road before – thought that it was all healed and then it'd re-infected. I don't want to get too excited, or too happy, until we know for sure.

9 May 2013

Finally, 14 days after I started treating Rich with the oil and the kefir, the nurse turned up again, with a piece of paper in her hand.

'Where is he?' she asked.

'Out on his tractor,' I admitted. The nurse laughed out loud. It *was* funny, and I laughed with her – after all, how ill could he be, if the nurse who came to treat him couldn't even find him, because he was out working?

She shook the paper at me.

'He's clear. The swab came back negative.'

I blinked hard a few times, to clear the mist that had suddenly come over my eyes.

'All clear?'

'All clear.'

She came around the table and enfolded me in a hard hug, the crisp blue of her uniform crinkling against my cheek.

'Well done,' she said.

15 June 2013

Rich continues to improve; he's gaining flesh and colour. The wound is completely closed, and it remains dry and healed. Hard to believe – still hard to trust – but I'm trusting it more, every day that he stays safe and well.

I wonder, was it really that essential oil combination that did the trick? Together with the probiotic oil? Or was it just a coincidence? How can I find out?

Glorying in the sight of Rich walking across the farmyard, tall as a tree, striding out the way he used to....

Later... The question is really starting to nag me now – what really did make Rich better? I have the name of a testing laboratory, MCS Laboratories: the one I used to safety assess my skin cream.

The technical manager there is named Angus, a lovely man. I phoned him and put my question to him. Was there a way to test the essential oil blend that I'd used on Rich? To find out if it really was what worked?

Angus assured me that such a test existed, and was fairly straightforward to perform. It would be expensive, he said, but I don't care – I simply have to know. He talked me through the process of downloading a test request form off the MCS website.

'What's the oil called?' he asked. I could hear his pen scratching over the phone as he made notes.

'Umm...' I considered. Not Chuckling Goat Oil – that made it sound like something unpleasant secreted by a goat. 'CG Oil?'

'Fair enough,' Angus said. And so CG Oil is born!

4 July 2013

I've been waiting anxiously for the results of the test to come back – seems like that's all I do these days. Not as tense as waiting for Rich's results to arrive, but pretty darn curious all the same. Like waiting for exam results, to see how you've done.

I've phoned Angus repeatedly to check on the process, and I'm sure he must be sick to death of me by now.

'We have to culture the bugs,' he explained patiently. 'If you want the oil tested against pathogens, we have to grow the correct pathogens first.'

6 July 2013

Finally, the results are here.

CG Oil is active against MRSA, at a dilution of .05 per cent. Turns out it's also active against E. coli, salmonella and campylobacter.

'Is that good?' I asked Angus.

'That's very good,' he replied.

Sitting outside with my laptop at the picnic table, enjoying a golden sunrise spilling over the hills. Very quiet, just the rush of the trees and some birdsong.

Rich is getting better, growing stronger by the day. His wound is completely healed.

And things are getting very interesting. The fact that the CG Oil is made from food grade ingredients and can potentially be eaten, inhaled, and used on skin makes it interesting to the Welsh Assembly government, who are now working with us on developing further applications of the oil. The Food Standards Agency is potentially interested to see how well the oil works against campylobacter. We're also working with Swansea University to do more advanced testing of both our kefir and the CG Oil.

And Fortnum & Mason – the famous 300-year-old London department store – is going to launch our probiotic skin care!

After the *Daily Mail* rated our oatmeal and honey soap nine out of 10, I plucked up my courage and sent the article to the most prestigious stores in the UK: Harrods, Selfridges and Fortnum & Mason. Straight for the top, I reasoned. It's a crazy shot in the dark anyhow, so why not?

But then Elizabeth Cook, the new buyer who'd just taken control of the Bath and Beauty department at Fortnum's, phoned me out of the blue. It seemed that she loved our products, and would like to stock our line. (As if we had a 'line'. Hah!) Could I come to London for a meeting to discuss?

By the strangest coincidence, I was on a train into London at the very moment I received the call. I was taking Joli in to put her on the plane to go and see her American relatives, as she does every summer.

I texted back that I could indeed make the meeting, and it was arranged for the next day, after I'd put Joli on the plane. I always take Joli a day early, and we stay in a hotel overnight and see a West End show. It's become a tradition – a way of coping with the grim reality of the six-hour train trip, and also to buffer the sadness of Joli going away for an entire month.

I told Joli what had just happened, and we held hands and bounced up and down in our seats, screaming soundlessly for a few minutes. Then I sat back and started to think feverishly. No appropriate clothes for a meeting at Fortnum & Mason, no soap samples with me, no time to ring Rich and have him ship samples by next day post, as it was already late afternoon. How the hell was I going to pull this off?

But I wasn't going to miss this meeting. It would be months before I could justify the expense of another trip into London, and even one day away from Rich, leaving the weight of the farm on his shoulders, was too much.

That evening, Joli and I went to see *Jersey Boys*, which we adored. I put her on the plane the next day, and clung to her before that horrible moment where she disappeared off through security, accompanied by the Virgin Atlantic representative. The airline has a great system in place for flying unaccompanied minors – you check the young people in at one end, and only a designated person with photo ID can collect them at the other end. A Virgin rep actually flies with them. Joli's been doing it since she was small, and she loves it.

So I watched her go, and cried, and then went to buy myself the traditional post-goodbye Krispy Kreme.

I had a problem. A meeting at Fortnum & Mason in six hours' time, to pitch a skincare line that didn't exist, and no samples. What do I always turn to in a crisis? Research.

I raced over to the pay-as-you-go computer terminals and feverishly plugged in my credit card. Not even sure what I was looking for. Natural skin care, natural health – maybe a spa?

I found something on the first page, a natural skincare line that used aromatherapy oils. Bingo. I use aromatherapy oils, too. But I have something they don't have – goat's milk. And now, after my experience with Rich, I know something else – kefir is magic for the skin. My magic ingredient.

I noted the address of the spa and set out on the Tube. Two hours later, I walked into the tiny spa, bought a sample bag of their products, turned around and walked out. Back onto the Tube. At Fortnum & Mason in Piccadilly, I allowed the doorman to swing open the massive mahogany and brass door, and told him (rather grandly) that I had a meeting there. He looked at me doubtfully, but let me in.

I walked up the red-carpeted staircase, past the intimidating oil paintings on the walls, and sat in the velvet wing chair placed there for visitors like myself. I wasn't wearing high heels and a suit, true, but my travel clothes would have to do.

When I was finally called into the meeting room, it looked like a newspaper office – terminals everywhere and people busily rushing around. Elizabeth Cook was young and charming and shook my hand enthusiastically.

I put my bag of purchased samples (beautifully wrapped, thank goodness!) down on the table in front of her.

'Everything they can do, we can do better,' I said, with confidence that I didn't feel. 'They use aromatherapy? We do too. But we have something that they don't have. Our products have goat's milk in them – and it's probiotic.'

'I'm listening,' she said.

So I told her the story of Rich, and his close escape, and how I learned to put kefir into soaps and skin creams.

She agreed that Fortnum & Mason would launch our line – of three creams and six soaps! – and I went home on the train floating on a cloud. I treated myself to a first-class ticket, clutching my lucky bag of purchased samples in my hands and refusing to allow myself to get worried about the fact that I'd just sold a line of products that didn't exist.

Yet.

A big spread about our battle with MRSA came out in *The Sun* daily newspaper, and we got a lot of publicity. The phone is ringing off the hook, and orders are flying in. NutriCentre in London wants to launch all our products, including the kefir and the coconut kefir. (Which I did, finally, get right!)

So, miracle after miracle.

But, sitting here at the picnic table in the sun, I can see the most important miracle of all. My Rich, in his denim shirt, sunburned and windswept, on his tractor in the field below me. Healthy and strong and alive.

Silver sun over the sea makes my chest ache, like someone is taking a soup spoon to my ribs.

It's funny, but in the wake of Fortnum & Mason's offer to stock our products, Rich and I decided that I should come in from the barn and devote all my time to product development. Or rather, I decided – and announced it – and he agreed. I'm sure that's how he would describe it, anyway!

We've been doing that for a few weeks now, and I must admit that, in the beginning, I loved it. It was luxurious to lie in bed while Rich got up to milk; lovely to have breakfast with Benji and take him to school. I did feel more energetic, I must admit. I did come home from the school run raring to go, whipping up multiple batches of soap before noon.

But...

Today Rich had a doctor's appointment in the morning, and so I went out to milk as I used to. Pulled on my striped wellies, stomped outside with the beautiful and talented Rosie Kitty – mother of all kittens and true boss of the barn – at my heels. (Rosie Kitty always waits for me at the door to walk me to the barn. There have been only two occasions when she wasn't there – when she was giving birth to her kittens, and when she was deathly ill. Otherwise, she's there. Always.)

In the barn, all was just as it used to be. Turn on the water heater, flick on the radio, swing the yellow bucket down and put it under the tap, turn the water to start filling it for later.

Fill the food bowls, sling them onto the milking stands, turn on the milking machine, let the first two ladies out of the pen to begin the hour-long dance of goats, milk and machine.

It was all so familiar. And yet I'd been gone for weeks, and it felt strange to be back – the goats looked at me reproachfully, and even Rosie Kitty seemed to be struggling to get back to our old, easy camaraderie. The big lead milker, Juliet, rubbed her head on my sleeve, over and over, and almost wouldn't let me get up. I saw a few goats with overgrown hooves that needed trimming. Patsy needed worming; I was sure of it. And we'd run out of beet shreds and no-one had replaced them, as it's usually my job.

I felt sad, and a little hollow, about all these things. I'd missed out on so much, and the life of the barn had carried on without me. Like looking at a child that I'd neglected, I felt guilty.

And then I realized that I *need* to be out in the barn. The goats need me and I need them. This is what I do; this is what keeps me honest. I could stay inside, and make fancy skin creams for fancy shops, and type on the computer, and it would be like living anywhere. I wouldn't have my hands on my own lovely goats, or my arms wrapped around this farm. I would be staying here, like a lodger – like the holidaymakers who stay in the cottage. But I wouldn't be *living* here.

Living, for me, requires a more passionate, energetic involvement. Living here means getting up and getting out into the barn in the early morning and doing the milking. And that's all there is to it.

So, I may be a little more tired. The products may be developed a little more slowly. And the paperwork may suffer. But the heart of this place is out there, in the barn, with the goats. And that's where I need to be.

25 July 2013

We've come so far in just six months. Now it's time to pay the piper. It's all very well coming up with lovely imaginary product lines, but now I'm going to have to produce the actual goods.

And there's no money to buy the jars and packaging that we need to get everything up to the specification that Fortnum & Mason require. We're going to have to sell Rich's motorcycle, and everything else we can lay our hands on – including some of the goats – to raise the cash to buy the jars and bottles for skin cream.

Is this what's known in business as 'problems with scaling'? I've no idea where the money will come from. I'm just going to have to pull a rabbit out of a hat somewhere. But what kind of rabbit, and which hat, I really couldn't say. I just refuse to believe that, having accomplished this dream of having a wonderful door open for us, we're not going to be able to afford to walk through it, for lack of seed money. Something will come along – it must!

We need bar codes... how does one go about getting a bar code? I'll have to figure this out in the very near future. The designer working on the packaging is waiting to hear, so that he can get the artwork to the printer. The probiotic bottle cleaner man is waiting to hear, so that he can reserve us time in the factory. And not only do I not have a clue what to do, I don't even know who to ask!

mcs
laboratories limited

Units 8 & 9 Rock Mill Business Park, The Dale
Stoney Middleton, Hope Valley, S32 4TF
Telephone: (01433) 639999
Fax: (01433) 639947

info@mcslabs.co.uk
www.mcslabs.co.uk

Chuckling Goat
Glynmelyn,
Brynhoffnant. Llandysul
SA44 6DS
FAO: Shann Jones

Order No:	
Date Received:	05.11.13
Date Tested:	11.11.13
Date Reported:	11.12.13
Report No:	75M31B

- Certificate of Analysis -

Test:	Minimum Inhibitory Concentration (MIC) determination using a solid dilution method
Method:	TMMCS5
Samples:	CG Oil (C.G.O.)
Modifications:	Test organisms selected were *S aureus* (MRSA), *E coli* & *Salmonella typhimurium*

Results:

% V/V product	Growth (+) or No Growth (-) of test organisms					
	S aureus (MRSA)		E coli		Salm typhimurium	
	L.O.	C.G.O	L.O.	C.G.O	L.O.	C.G.O
6.25	-	-	-	-	-	-
3.13	-	-	-	-	-	-
1.56	-	-	-	-	-	-
0.78	-	-	-	-	-	-
0.40	-	-	-	-	-	-
0.20	-	-	-	-	-	-
0.10	-	-	-	-	-	-
0.05	-	~	-	-	~	~
Zero	+	+	+	+	+	+

Determined MIC values %V/V

Sample	S aureus (MRSA)	E coli	Salm typhimurium
CG Oil	<0.05	<0.05	<0.05

Comments:
The results apply only to the sample(s) tested.

A S Malcolm BSc
Technical Manager

MCS report 75M31B
MCS Laboratories Limited - Registered in England & Wales – Company No.08121022

Independent microbiology laboratory report showing that CG Oil is active against MRSA, E. coli, salmonella and Campylobacter.

Still, we'll work it out in the end. We always do. Having survived what we've survived, the rest is cake. It feels like our luck has finally turned, even without money.

The weather has been blissfully hot and sunny for week upon week now – Rich says he hasn't seen anything like it since he was a boy. Blue skies, golden fields… we had the ultimate luxury of getting all the hay in, with time left over to spare.

I have moulds full of pale green tea-tree goat's milk kefir soap curing on the kitchen table – part of the new probiotic skincare line that we're creating for Fortnum & Mason. It smells like heaven – sharp and herby, like the goat's milk soap, but even nicer.

Somehow the goat's milk kefir just does magic things in the soap. The skin cream works perfectly to cure loads of problems – it seems to work on eczema, psoriasis, rosacea, spots – even cracked heels! We've yet to try it on anything that it fails to clear up. This is my favourite bit – the experimenting and making things from the milk the goats give us. And my lovely, brilliant, wonderful mother is helping us with a bridging loan, enough to allow us to buy the jars and bottles and labels we need for the Fortnum & Mason launch. Bless her! Thank goodness for family!

So it's full speed ahead… We've come such a way – such a very, very long way. But we made it through all that darkness, in the end, and that's what matters. We're together. Rich is still alive. He's healthy and strong and back on his tractor. And I've learned such a lot. Not lessons I would have volunteered for, certainly. But as a result, magical doors have opened for me that I never imagined to be possible. Truly, I must be the luckiest woman in the world....

Epilogue

Rich pulled his beautifully cut Harris tweed jacket, specially imported from Edinburgh at some trouble and expense, over his carefully ironed, brand new shirt. He tied his silk tie, put on the lovely leather brogues borrowed from his brother Rhys especially for the occasion (having been forbidden his beloved cowboy boots), and scowled at me.

Rich hates dressing up.

But he looked natty, handsome and exactly what he was – a prosperous Welsh farmer going to meet HRH The Prince of Wales.

I scrambled into my own hastily assembled outfit. Black jacket and trousers, silk blouse, pearl earrings – the goats wouldn't recognize me! And then we were off.

In the car on the way, I pored over the list of etiquette do's and don'ts for meeting royalty – as an American, I'd never really considered the ins and outs of curtsying while wearing trousers. Wait for HRH to speak first. Don't offer to shake hands unless he initiates it. Your Royal Highness is the preferred address the first time, and Sir thereafter. And, most important of all, no inappropriate jokes or remarks about other members of the royal family. Hmmm...

I sighed and looked sideways at Rich, who was driving grimly and staring straight ahead, wearing his Braveheart face. I supposed I was lucky, really, that he wasn't showing up wearing skins, with blue streaks painted across his cheekbones. As a patriotic Welshman, it was a stretch for him even to consent to show up today to chitchat with English royalty. I'd no hopes whatsoever of getting him to bow.

But I had no such scruples! I was just plain excited. We'd been contacted by the Cambrian Mountain Initiative, an organization inspired by the Prince to promote rural products. We've been to a couple of meetings, and now we'd been offered this chance to meet HRH.

I didn't really know what to think about it, to be honest. The chance of actually getting to talk with the Prince himself seemed pretty remote. But at the very least, I thought, I'll be in the same room as him, and I suppose that's something that not many people can say!

When we arrived at the Y Talbot Hotel in Tregaron, West Wales, we could see police ringing the building, and dressed-up members of the group were beginning to drift through the doors. We parked the car, found an entrance and joined the swarm of about 50 nervous people. There was a buffet lunch – I tried to avoid anything that might drip onto my shirt-front – and a business meeting first: slides and explanations of what would happen with the group in the upcoming year.

We'd brought a sample bag of our Chuckling Goat raw goat's milk soap for HRH, without any real hope that we'd be allowed to give it to him. Surely security concerns would forbid such things? But when I asked the lady who'd organized the day whether it was possible, she said to go ahead, that people quite often gave things to the Prince. (Another thing we discovered – never say, 'he' or 'him'. And apparently it's terrible vulgar to use first names – 'Prince Charles' is completely out of the question!)

Then a buzz started going around the room that HRH was on his way. Someone asked us to get to our feet and stand near the door. We were arranged in groups according to farming interest – the butchers all in one group, small producers in another.

As we make soap (non-edibles) we were put together with a lady who makes wool. We were told not to move, but not to look as though we were standing waiting, either. We tried our best to accommodate these conflicting directions. A gentleman in an extremely well-cut suit came around and said politely, 'His Royal Highness will be holding a cup of tea, but he won't drink from it unless you are also holding one. So may I suggest that you get yourself a cup of tea?'

As this was clearly more than just a suggestion, I did as I was told. Rich doesn't drink tea, and in full rebel mode now, flatly refused to get one. I began to panic. There were too many things to hold – how was I going to manage a cup and saucer and a sample bag of soap, plus curtsy, shake hands (don't initiate hand shaking, but be ready to respond if HRH seems to want to shake your hand), and remember everything else? I shoved the sample bag into Rich's hand, and prayed I wouldn't spill tea all over myself and HRH.

I muttered to the wool lady standing next to us that HRH must think that everyone in the world has sweaty palms – I certainly did!

Finally, The Person In Question came into the room. Contrary to the impression I had from seeing him on television, where he appears tall and austere, HRH is charismatic, charming and very warm. It was strange, finally seeing a face in person that you've seen so many times in print and on screen.

HRH spoke to the butchers' groups next to us for a long time, while we fidgeted and tried not to stare or eavesdrop. When he finally moved on to us, he was warm and pleasant, leaning forwards into the conversation, his voice pitched low and casual. I managed to curtsy and say, 'Your Royal Highness'. Unsurprisingly, Rich didn't bow or bend the knee. Half horrified and half quite proud of him, I hoped no-one would come and drag him off for committing treason.

'Have you come far today?' HRH asked. (I smiled to myself – he had no idea how far we'd really come. Or the adventures we'd survived along the way!) He looked at my name badge, probing for a hint of who we were, a suggestion for the next topic. What a burden, to lead conversations with 50 over-awed, nervous strangers! I didn't envy his job at that moment.

Our name badges identified us as 'Chuckling Goat'. HRH seized on the clue. 'And what do you do with the goats?' he asked. 'Well, Your Royal Highness, now there's a leading question,' Rich said. I held my breath – no impertinent remarks! But HRH laughed, and it was all right after that.

We gave him the soap, which was handed back to the private secretary hovering behind the royal shoulder, and he asked all about it, with what seemed like genuine interest. 'Tell me, does it also cure wrinkles?' he asked.

'Well,' Rich said, 'my wife here is really 93 years old!' (Luckily I'm still *just* young enough for that to be funny!)

We chatted for what seemed like a long time, but was in reality probably five or six minutes, and then HRH smiled and thanked us and moved gracefully on.

Later we got a lovely letter from HRH's private secretary, thanking us for the 'gift of Chuckling Goat toiletries' and saying that they had been 'safely transported' to the Prince's Welsh home at Llwynywermod, just outside Brecon Beacons National Park, where they 'will be greatly enjoyed'.

I imagined a liveried butler, trotting along with our soaps on a silver salver, 'transporting' them. I smiled, and carefully folded the letter back into its thick, creamy envelope.

Well, imagine that... our own soaps, made on the farmhouse kitchen table, being used and enjoyed by royalty.

I went out to the barn, to show the letter to the goats. 'Well done, you goats,' I said. 'You amazing, beautiful goats. You made it all happen, didn't you? You taught me everything I needed to know.' They just winked at me and chuckled. They knew.

~~~~~~~~~~~

Acknowledgements

I'm a late bloomer, and living proof that life really does start after 40 – I was 41 before I met the man for me, and 47 before I encountered the publishing house where I always wanted to be.

Hay House is a collection of the most fantastic, genuine people, and working with this group of experts has been a revelation – *this* is how publishing should be, and so rarely is!

My heartfelt thanks to Reid Tracy, who saw instantly the future vision of what Chuckling Goat could be, and reached out his hand to make it happen. Talk about waving a wand and saying that we shall go to the ball! Humble and profound gratitude, for all the myriad of possibilities you've brought within reach for us.

Michelle Pilley – lovely, wise, kind and extraordinarily professional. If I could pick up a pen and draw the perfect mentor, it would be Michelle. Thank you for all your guidance!

Debra Wolter, who edited this manuscript with a touch so deft and gentle that I actually enjoyed the process – unheard of! And was patient with my crazy schedule while I tried to keep all my millions of plates spinning in the air. Thank you, Debra.

Jo Burgess and Ruth Tewkesbury, who came to visit us and became a part of the virtual farm team, forever more... The goats send their regards!

Sincere thanks to all the HH team who offered their expertise and put their hands on this project throughout the process – Leanne Sui Anastasi, Julie Oughton, Michelle Cameron, Tom Cole. Fab professionals, every one.

Thanks to my agent, Bonnie Nadell, who has worked with me for oh, what is it now – a quarter of a century! Since we were both young and running amok in San Francisco. Thank you for your faith in me, Bonnie – and for your ongoing patience, support, and unerring ability to sort out the wheat from the chaff.

Grateful thanks to Ann and Geoff Napier of Cygnus Books, who saw the possibilities and introduced me to Hay House in the first place. Never have matchmakers been so appreciated!

Of course, I must thank my family, who mean the world to me. What a journey we've come on together!

To Rich, who bravely took on a stroppy single mum and her two children, and loved her into a truly cherished and contented wife and mother. Your patience is always a revelation to me.

To the memory of Taid, who welcomed my children into his heart, and gave us the gift of his laughter and his beautiful farm by the sea.

To Ceris and Elly, who invited us wholeheartedly into their lives, shared their dad with me, and didn't complain once as their home was invaded by younger siblings. You two are such beautiful girls – lucky me, to get to add you to my family the easy way!

To Joli and Benji, who came along for the whole journey. Sorry to drag you guys around so much – and apologies for taking such a long time to crack the whole family thing! You are both fabulous, and I can't wait to see what you do in the future.

A resounding thank you goes to my mother and father, Ann and Don Nix, who floated our leaky canoe over some very dangerous rocks during times when we would've gone under without their help. Without your assistance, we wouldn't still be paddling.

Thanks to Dr Natasha Campbell-McBride, whose seminal work on Gut and Psychology Syndrome and the GAPS diet led us to kefir in the first place. It is impossible, in my opinion, to overstate the importance of this work and its ability to change the world, one patient at a time. Her brilliance is inspiring, and her encouragement gave us our very first start. Thank you, Dr Natasha!

And finally, I'm forever grateful to Janey Lee Grace, bestselling author and bright star of the natural product world. As a passionate mentor for holistic businesses, this is a lady who proves every day that business truly can be heart-centred.

Janey has inspired, encouraged and assisted our little family-run concern through some very dark days – and it was entirely due to her insistence that this book was ever completed and published. Thank you, Janey – every business should be lucky enough to have your coaching!

ABOUT THE AUTHOR

Neil Buckland

Shann Nix Jones was the ultimate American city girl until she fell in love with a Welsh farmer at the age of 41. Shann and her husband, Rich, realized that they could do something extraordinary when they started to work with goats' milk and used it to heal their son's eczema. They decided to quit their respective day jobs, and try to make a go of the goats' milk business full time.

In April 2011, the couple launched their online business, Chuckling Goat, selling health-enhancing soaps, creams and probiotic kefir drinks which they make by hand on the farm. The launch was a huge success, and today their award-winning homemade products are available all over the United Kingdom. They now have 55 goats who have become like members of the family.

www.chucklinggoat.co.uk

We hope you enjoyed this Hay House book. If you'd like to receive our online catalog featuring additional information on Hay House books and products, or if you'd like to find out more about the Hay Foundation, please contact:

Hay House, Inc., P.O. Box 5100, Carlsbad, CA 92018-5100
(760) 431-7695 or (800) 654-5126
(760) 431-6948 (fax) or (800) 650-5115 (fax)
www.hayhouse.com® • www.hayfoundation.org

Published in Australia by: Hay House Australia Pty. Ltd.,
18/36 Ralph St., Alexandria NSW 2015
Phone: 612-9669-4299 • *Fax:* 612-9669-4144
www.hayhouse.com.au

Published in the United Kingdom by: Hay House UK, Ltd.,
The Sixth Floor, Watson House, 54 Baker Street, London W1U 7BU
Phone: +44 (0)20 3927 7290 • *Fax:* +44 (0)20 3927 7291
www.hayhouse.co.uk

Published in India by: Hay House Publishers India,
Muskaan Complex, Plot No. 3, B-2, Vasant Kunj, New Delhi 110 070
Phone: 91-11-4176-1620 • *Fax:* 91-11-4176-1630
www.hayhouse.co.in

Access New Knowledge.
Anytime. Anywhere.

Learn and evolve at your own pace
with the world's leading experts.

www.hayhouseU.com